FRENCH INTROSPECTIVES
FROM MONTAIGNE TO ANDRÉ GIDE.

FRENCH INTROSPECTIVES

FROM MONTAIGNE TO
ANDRÉ GIDE

BY

P. MANSELL JONES

*Professor of French in the University
College of North Wales, Bangor*

GREENWOOD PRESS, PUBLISHERS
WESTPORT, CONNECTICUT

"*Introspections*—heureux à tous égards, disait-il, car, même totalement incompris, on ne peut se méprendre sur la direction *intus*, sur le *in*...." (From a conversation with André Gide.)

CHARLES DU BOS:
Extraits d'un Journal (1908–1928)

Originally published in 1937
by Cambridge University Press

First Greenwood Reprinting 1970

Library of Congress Catalogue Card Number 73-95107

SBN 8371-3113-8

Printed in the United States of America

CONTENTS

Preface   *page* vii

I   The Limits of Literary Introspection   1

II   Montaigne's Self-Portraiture and the Definition of the Essays   22

III   Judgment and Relation in the Essays of Montaigne   34

IV   The Inner Life of a Philosopher: Maine de Biran's *Journal Intime*   42

V   Sénancour's *Obermann*   57

VI   Some Romantic Poets   69

VII   The Failure of Amiel   77

VIII   The Paradox of Literary Introspection   92

IX   In Search of the Self   103

PREFACE

AUTOBIOGRAPHY is in the fashion, in favour with authors and publishers, popular, to judge by lending-library stocks, with a large proportion of the reading public. Yet it would be a mistake to think that autobiography, especially when serious and intimate, is a type of literature to everyone's liking. Few can resist the attraction of a contemporary's exposure of himself —how he made his fortune or met his fate, why he deserted a party or divorced a wife; and if he can tell us the "secret" of these things he has a reason to be heard. But apart from appeals to curiosity and fillips to prurience, critical discussion of the subject yields only too often to irrelevant personal allusions and pious disapproval.

People of taste usually prefer what is objective in form, if not in spirit; realists, they shudder at realism in the first person. The facile or the profound exhibitionism involved in confession or self-portrayal is equally abhorrent to them. They are irritated by the indiscretions which make the confession genuine. They pounce upon self-criticisms and use them triumphantly to dispose of the matter. This may be why autobiography as an art receives so little recognition; why with a specimen to review a serious judge will concentrate on the life, not on the book; why from Montaigne and Rousseau to Gide, Wells and Middleton Murry, the experience renews itself: to publish one's life is to invite reproach for having lived it. The man who writes about himself is a prig, a bore, a sentimentalist, a megalomaniac, a cynical self-adulator or a propagandist for his own *mauvaises mœurs*, before he is allowed to be an autobiographer. Charged with being an apologist, defending instead of arraigning himself, he is grudged credit for having made an effort to understand or explain himself.

Criticism of this type of literature remains, as a result, largely a department of moral or social censure. It may always be so: the type invites it. For what should (such) a book teach but the art of living? Dr Johnson's question must be met with the statement that to extract and present the lesson are affairs of psychology and literary art. It is one thing to blame the autobiographer for the life he has lived; it is another to consider his work in relation to the defects and failures in which it may have originated, or which may have forced or modified its development. I assume that a man intent on self-examination and gifted in self-disclosure can make a distinctive contribution which perpetually evades the verdict, gratuitous or verifiable, passed on his behaviour.

Not that we have to accept his evaluations. In autobiography especially it is significance that counts—significance of data, emphasis, "revelation"; and it is we who judge these things by our own standards. Ultimately, no doubt, the nature of the life and the quality of the person cannot be kept out of the account. But they should be brought in to confirm not to prejudice the verdict.

The real art of the man who writes about himself is to arrange for publication at a favourable moment posthumously. Distance softens the importunity of the

"I", and time permits another egoist to discover a genius.

Even that may be too early for judgment.

The nucleus of this book is a short series of relatively independent studies, not designed to present an exhaustive treatment or to sustain a thesis. A common thread, or at least a single intention, runs through them and will, I hope, explain the basis of selection. Put simply, it is the search for examples of introspection in a literature which is reputed to be rich in them.

The first chapter is concerned with distinctions. One of these it seems necessary to mention here, because it has determined my line of approach. It is a discrimination, which could be made absolute only in theory, between the introspective and other autobiographical types of literature. I suggest that most of what passes for autobiography is, in essence, biography written in the first person; while what the French call an "écrit intime" is not the record of a life, but essentially a study of the self.[1] I have chosen those specimens of the latter kind which seemed most deliberately and consistently intimate, those which might be expected to present, directly and unequivocally, the authentic results of a study of the self as practised by non-professionals of genius. These are surprisingly few. Even the exiguous group here represented—so scarce are examples of pure introspec-

[1] The rigidity of this distinction will be modified later. The difficulty is largely one of nomenclature. A slight acquaintance with the subject does, I think, show that we lack categories, descriptive and critical, adequate to the extent and variety of kinds roughly grouped under Autobiography or Memoirs. What attempts I have made to discriminate are tentative.

tion—contains one philosopher. But the philosophy of Maine de Biran seems to have proceeded from his habit of inspecting his own mind, and not *vice versa*. Another is not directly and unequivocally a diarist. His chief work, *Obermann*, I use as a foil, an example of the *faux intime*.

To deal adequately with the ultimate problem to which these studies obviously lead would require far more philosophy than I possess or am likely to acquire. The method I have adopted has been to watch at work a few artists in introspection and to attempt to judge them on their apparent merits and defects as amateurs. In encouragement and defence of this attitude it is comforting to recall that it was not for philosophers or for any kind of specialist, but for themselves as amateurs that these non-sectarian Solitaries kept watch with themselves and recorded (though perhaps in the last resort for other eyes after and like their own) the gains and losses they experienced in pursuit of their inner quest.

The more serious, not to say the more logical, of Introspectives must sooner or later inquire what they are in themselves. Stendhal asked this question, squatting on the steps of St Peter's on the morning of his fiftieth birthday. Amiel turned it over off and on for forty years. Montaigne, despite his nonchalance, confessed himself to be at all times "preparé environ ce que je puis estre". I do not pretend to know what answer they found, or even what each self-interrogator meant by the "moi" he was at once interrogating and looking for. But it will be agreed, I think, that in each case the question was not, "*How* do I know myself?" or "*What* is introspection?" An epistemologist might therefore be thought ready to despise them. Most probably he would not. The gift of introspection does not seem to have been so lavishly distributed among Western Man as is apparently the talent for philosophising. And the philosopher would no doubt be wise enough to respect any one whose greater experiential claim could be characterised in Amiel's words, when, registering defeat at all other points, he wrote in his Journal: "Ici tu peux passer du rang d'amateur à celui de spécialité." This claim does not of course contradict what has been said above. By "spécialité" Amiel meant not an acquired specialism, but a special gift developed to a superior degree.

Having recognised the precedence of the philosopher in matters appertaining to knowledge of the Self, I may now express the hope, without too heavy a feeling of presumption, that a few of his kind will allow themselves to be included among those to whom I offer no deep argument of my own, but some observations prompted by a variety of examples which I have found fascinating and in which English readers may find, along with much that is familiar, much perhaps that is new. This is my excuse for having frequently attempted translation. But there is French too for those who like it. Short passages have usually been given in the original form, which has always been kept when the style seemed significant.

Of the friends who have helped with criticism and advice I should like especially to thank Professor F. C. Green and Mr F. W. Stokoe of Cambridge, and Professor J. L. André Barbier of Aberystwyth. Mr T. S. Eliot has allowed the inclusion of an essay on Amiel which appeared in the *Criterion* for October 1935. Similar permission has been given by Mr R. A. Scott-James in respect of an article called "The Paradox of Literary Introspection" from the *London Mercury* for September of that year. The Librairie Plon of Paris has given consent to the use I have made of passages from a recent edition of Maine de Biran's *Journal Intime*, published by that house.

P. M. J.

Cambridge 1937

CHAPTER I

THE LIMITS OF LITERARY INTROSPECTION

I

FEW things in literature are as rare as introspection—as rare, that is, if we decide to give the word a definite meaning. The Shorter Oxford Dictionary defines it as "the action of looking within or into one's own mind". By introspection for the purpose of this inquiry I mean that, or as I should prefer to put it, the disinterested investigation of a mind by itself. This would preclude the systematic approach of the philosopher as well as the technical approach of the psychologist. It is advisable also for the delimitation of our field to dissociate at once other mental activities, such as objective reflection, speculation, reverie, rumination, fantasy or dreams, all of which have passed muster, even with devotees, as "introspection". Some of these activities may rival and even surpass the latter in the light they can throw on the mind of a person under their control. Recent tendencies in psychology make it unwise to assert that what a person reveals of himself by direct conscious analysis is necessarily superior in value or importance to what is indirectly revealed of him in less deliberate and less conscious ways. It is not my purpose to evaluate. I simply propose as an axiom what is really a conclusion: that the best working definition of "introspection" applicable to the literary examples with which we shall here be concerned is the conscious examination of a mind by itself.

Such delimitation has obvious dangers and may need support before it can be accepted as a working basis. Our examples are to be drawn from French introspective literature. It is therefore appropriate to begin by acknowledging a couple of serious studies of a semi-literary character, which have appeared in France within the last decade and which touch this subject closely. I refer to M. Jean Prévost's *Essai sur l'Introspection* (1927) and *De la Personnalité* by M. Ramon Fernandez (1928), both published by the "Sans Pareil" Press. Each draws the depths of personality with a broader and more searching net than I can pretend to manipulate. But the ocean of the self is wide enough to permit one to angle on its shores, while deep-sea fishers operate at a distance, bringing prodigies to light. I shall regard the works of these two investigators as standards or models to gauge the limits I have set my subject and to justify the way in which it has been handled.

M. Prévost himself deals mainly with the limits of introspection, as the general editor of the series points out. The "theory of introspection" which he examines is based on features common to all types of mind. It is, he admits, abstract. He seems inclined to make it include any type of thinking in which the mind is not occupied with external objects. M. Fernandez, on the other hand, is mainly interested in the definition of Personality. The introspective approach to its secrets is only part of his concern. Tacitly he agrees with M. Prévost that introspection has its limits. Both are impressed with its uncertainty or its insecurity as a process for getting at the truth of personality. Both are severe judges of the introspective method and habit, regarded from a scientific or from a moral standpoint. But while they are sensitive to the dangers and defects of the inactive state as a means of self-knowing, they agree that withdrawal from the outer world is a *sine qua non*. "For introspection", writes M. Prévost, "one must suppose the observer inactive, or at least with no other object than himself." This state is foreign to most people; it is an "état rare" (p. 26). For M. Fernandez, too, introspection begins "when the subject is interested in events which do not demand from him an immediate active response; that is, when, being no longer forced to know himself through action, he is at leisure to consider his intimate consciousness as a sort of book or mirror in which his moral features are being inscribed" (p. 113).

These quotations provide what may be called our premises. But before we proceed, another important distinction requires to be made. "Soyons juste!" exclaims M. Paul Valéry, "Le seul catholicisme a approfondi la 'vie intérieure'" (*Cahier B*, p. 56). Can we avoid referring to religious literature? Such an exclusion would indeed be arbitrary, had we in view a general investigation into the nature of introspection as variously exemplified in literatures of all types, mystical and philosophical, as well as "secular". The secular, however, must be our field, not only for the arbitrary reason of fixing practical limits to what might otherwise become an endless inquiry, but more pertinently because "secular", or as we shall call it "literary", introspection is, or appears to be, if not a gratuitous act, less consciously motivated, at least, than the religious variety.

The latter depends more or less directly on an effort towards examination of the self imposed by, or in view of, an end which Christianity has called the salvation of the soul. This end is extrinsic and ulterior to the purely intellectual pursuit of self-comprehension. But to affirm that is to raise some of the worst difficulties of delimitation. Is introspection ever a purely intellectual pursuit? Is it ever unmotivated? How near can it come to self-comprehension? A hornet's nest of interrogations!— some of which we shall try to deal with in the sequel; others we shall, in the interests of our purpose, evade if we can. For there is still one more set of distinctions which we cannot ignore, and they bring us to the heart of the subject.

In autobiographical literature itself there are many allied types which must be kept distinct from the truly introspective. Of one of these Benedetto Croce wrote in his *Autobiography*: "Memoirs are the chronicle of one's life and the lives of the men with whom one has worked or whom one has seen and known, and events in which one has taken part; and people write them in the hope of preserving for posterity important facts which otherwise would be forgotten." Clearly memoirs approximate to history, not to introspection; while the vast majority of "lives" must be classed as private or family history. It has already been suggested that most of what passes for autobiography could better be described as biography written in the first person. One is familiar with the external sequence which the author's wife or valet or an observant friend might have served

LIMITS OF LITERARY INTROSPECTION

up as a memorial. In contrast to such *reportage* a *journal intime* is, I contend, not the record of a life but essentially a study of the self. Yet the most personal of journals contain much that is external, descriptive, "autobiographical" in the accepted sense; and most good autobiographies have remarkable episodes of self-analysis. The distinction cannot be pressed too far in that direction. It may, however, be resumed in another. An autobiography is a narrative composed after the event. Such intimate episodes as occur are, as a rule, analyses of motives recollected in tranquillity. It is difficult to think of a "life" of this kind which is not preponderantly a tissue of reminiscences. The journal, on the other hand, is contemporaneous by definition.

Nothing intended as *apology* can satisfy our requirements; though here again our limits threaten to become oppressive. If they exclude Rousseau's *Confessions* and the brilliant but external *Mémoires d'Outre-Tombe*, what of St Augustine's? And what of Newman's *Pro Vita Sua*? For Newman and Augustine cannot be disposed of under the religious category. Fortunately, neither was a Frenchman. Jean-Jacques however must detain us a moment.

Lytton Strachey considered that Rousseau had pushed the introspective method to its farthest limit. But where? In the Letters to Malesherbes or the Confessions, in the Reveries or the three Dialogues in which he pretends to judge himself?

Let us first remove an ambiguity. Certain passages in the Confessions which some critics denounce and others ignore seem to have given the author a reputation for introspection which is hard to justify. Introspection should be distinguishable from a type of intimate confession which is merely an indiscreet form of personal disclosure. The confidence may refer to habits not usually discussed and its interest may end there, not in new light thrown on the interior or the reality of the self. The confusion here arises from different connotations of the word "intimate".

Rousseau's solitude is a life of reverie lived apart from society and stimulated by contact with nature. It produces: (i) dreams of a better society mingled with memories of happy moments in his experience—"toutes les scènes de ma vie qui m'avaient laissé de doux souvenirs", and "toutes celles que mon cœur pouvait désirer encore"; (ii) emotional reactions to these dreams and memories—"sentiments exquis". Together these occupy the heart and mind of the solitary. But they imply only a superficial kind of self-knowledge. They constitute, rather, a mode of life which Rousseau loved to describe. His introspection never pierces their level. The account of his "état moral" given in the course of the Letters to Malesherbes is precisely an account of these experiences. The finest example of all is the fifth of the *Rêveries d'un promeneur solitaire*. But here we approach the heights of a new type of lyricism rather than the depths of introspection. Some critics might prefer to say, we approach the mirk of narcissism rather than the clarity of self-knowledge.

In the third Letter to Malesherbes, it is true, Rousseau passes momentarily beyond, but to arrive immediately at a feeling of emptiness ("vide"), which is itself a source of "jouissance". Every experience of the kind, in fact *every* experience, ends for Rousseau in a sentiment or a sensation, at best in an "étourdissante extase". The basic moods recur in all the "introspective" parts of his work: they are few and familiar. Far from increasing in the knowledge or revelation of the self, Rousseau evades self-scrutiny and indulges in descriptions of a limited set of moods. As descriptions they are incomparably successful, even when we remember Wordsworth's. But their motive is self-justification not self-comprehension. The loveliest of the Letters to Malesherbes is prompted by the wish to explain "les vrais motifs de ma retraite et de toute ma conduite". This it achieves. But do any of them, or the whole of his writings, justify the claim: "Personne au monde ne me connaît que moi seul. Vous en jugerez quand j'aurai tout dit"?[1]

It is obvious that a man may "confess" many things which have not required much searching of heart. Open Benjamin Constant's *Journal Intime*.[2] It begins in the year 1804. The friend of Mme de Staël, the enemy of Napoleon, is in exile at Weimar. He reads, writes and visits, goes to the theatre, dines with celebrities including Goethe. Most of the entries are brief, masterly annotations of the vicissitudes of an active, agitated existence. Not a touch of repose, hardly a trace of inwardness. This supreme egoist is simply not interested in the self. On

[1] In the second of the Dialogues, called *Rousseau juge de Jean-Jacques*, the author reproaches his critics with two faults of method: "Il faut rétrograder vers le temps où rien ne l'empêchait d'être lui-même, ou bien le pénétrer plus intimement, *intus et in cute*, pour y lire immédiatement les véritables dispositions de son âme." How far can Rousseau himself be said to have turned the "innocent eye" upon his youth or to have probed beneath his all too sensitive skin?

[2] Librairie Stock, 1928. Constant's early life is recorded in the *Cahier Rouge*, a vivid segment of autobiography, rich in escapades but devoid of intimacy.

his thirty-seventh birthday he writes: "...Ma vie ne m'a laissé que des souvenirs assez confus. Je ne m'intéresse guère plus à moi qu'aux autres" (p. 104). Yet one illuminating aside does at least show that Constant, publicist, politician, turncoat, gambler and philanderer as he was, had realised the difficulty of making the intimate point of view predominant. One evening he picks up his Journal and amuses himself with looking through what he has written. This is his comment: "...En commençant je m'étais promis de ne parler que pour moi, et cependant telle est l'influence de l'habitude de parler pour la galerie que quelquefois je me suis oublié. Bizarre espèce humaine qui ne peut jamais être complètement indépendante! Les autres sont les autres, et l'on ne fera jamais qu'ils soient 'soi'" (p. 119). A later birthday finds him again in a reminiscent mood. But this time the entry turns to comedy: "Aujourd'hui, 25 octobre 1811, j'ai quarante-quatre ans. Ai-je réellement bien employé ces deux tiers de ma vie? Tâchons de mieux faire! J'ai une belle-sœur aigre et sèche. Au fait, cela regarde mon beau-frère. Je n'ai pas mal travaillé. Mon livre avance. Charlotte est douce et bonne. Nous empaquetons pour aller à Göttingen. Déménagement abominable! Que de paquets j'ai déjà faits dans ma vie!" (p. 182).

The sequel sketches with incomparable verve the inner history of Constant's flight from Mme de Staël, his marriage with Charlotte von Hardenberg and his absurd passion for Mme Récamier; but it tells us little or nothing of what Benjamin makes of himself.

Let us return to graver consideraticns.

In this passage from Maine de Biran's Journal, already

introduced to English readers by Mr Aldous Huxley, we see the French philosopher drawing an acute distinction between the type of man who is capable of meditation and the type who is not. Maine de Biran is commenting on a thought of Pascal. "Would one not say", he asks, "that the removal of all causes of external sensation or amusement was enough to turn any individual into a deep thinker busy with self-analysis, with meditation on life and death and all that is most distressing in the condition of humanity? Yet, on the contrary, to meditate thus, after having deliberately withdrawn from all sources of impression, one must exert more effort and intellectual activity than is required to follow the course of all the affairs of life. The activity which makes us think of ourselves is only a mode of that activity which, according to Pascal, would prevent us thinking of ourselves by filling our mind with any other thing. Thus from the standpoint that all mental labour tends only to steal us from ourselves, we should only be thinking of ourselves to distract us from ourselves or to forget ourselves: strange and inexplicable contradiction. Remove all sensible impressions, all causes of movement, and there would be left a dreadful void, a nullity of existence, so to speak, for those who know and love only the life of sensations. But thought will fill this void or make it imperceptible for those who are accustomed to the intellectual life: even when they meditate on the nothingness of man, they would have a full life...."[1]

This distinction helps us with one more exclusion. But along with the sensationalist we must also dismiss the philosopher whom Maine de Biran thinks of as

[1] Maine de Biran, *Journal Intime*, ed. Valette-Monbrun, II, p. 56.

capable of filling the void left by the withdrawal from sensation. Philosophical meditation is not identical with introspection. This Biran seems to admit. It may lead a thinker as far from himself as sensation could. How far we shall see when we examine his Journal. For another example of the appropriation or application of the introspective method comparable in importance to his (though very different in kind), we must make a leap of a hundred years and drop from the study into the arena.

Maurice Barrès brilliantly exemplifies what might be called teleological or purposive self-analysis. His attitude and method are defined in the phrase, *Le culte du moi*. Under this head he grouped the three "romans idéologiques" with which he began. Contemporary protests against their obscurity induced him to prefix a synopsis which figures as the *Examen* in the definitive edition, and makes his intention clear: "Proposing to put into the form of a novel the conception people of our time arrive at of the universe, when their thought is their own and not a repetition of formulas found in their readings, I felt obliged to begin with a study of the Self..." (p. 14). The modern young man suffering from lack of energy and objective must learn to know himself, to distinguish his real interests, his instinctive direction, his own truth. Let him take his stand on the Self until an energetic person comes to reconstruct religion for him (pp. 40, 41).

The *Examen* abounds in precepts of self-analysis. But the works themselves are too indirect and symbolical in style to detain us. As the *Cahiers* show, Barrès was not an introspective by nature, but a man of action who had worked back to his own roots in order to devote himself effectively to radical reforms. The "culte du moi" is the first stage of an evolution which led through the "culte des morts" to the *Roman de l'énergie nationale* and the *Scènes et doctrines du nationalisme*—works which have their counterpart in the electoral campaign and the preaching of the *Revanche*. From the standpoint of the mood of the age, the career as a whole is a *reaction* from analysis.

M. Philippe Barrès, editing the *Cahiers*, has characterised their contents as "notes et observations". Into them Barrès poured "all the images of his childhood and youth, his treasure of reveries, pretty faces and twilight dreams" (I, p. 3); not for the sake of painting pictures of the past, but because he wished to realise the lessons he had derived from life, how he had matured and progressed. In this effort to sift healthy from unhealthy experiences and to estimate his obligations, we see him apply the pragmatic test to his own record: it was always the cult, not the *knowledge*, of the self which interested Barrès.

One of his models, it may be recalled, was Marie Bashkirtseff, the young Russian princess-turned-artist, the reputation of whose diary he did so much to establish. "À propos," she wrote in an intuitive moment, "très souvent je tâche de savoir ce que j'ai en face de moi-même, mais très caché, la vérité enfin." Then she adds: "Car tout ce que je pense, tout ce que je suis, est seulement extérieur..." (*Journal*, I, p. 39).

That sentence most autobiographers could apply to themselves. The tension of inward scrutiny makes too great a demand on concentration for any but a very few persons at rare moments of their experience to be capable of the necessary response. Why does the attention of even the most serious investigator of the self seem doomed to wander? Why should it deviate? What—when outer claims and clamours have ceased—diverts it from sustained scrutiny and progressive analysis?

II

For many acutely analytic minds the examination of the self is a painful and repugnant process. Mme Du Deffand finely adumbrated the attitude of such a mind in a letter to Maupertuis: "La réflexion apprend qu'il ne faut pas beaucoup réfléchir, et que pour vivre en paix il faut beaucoup s'occuper; et quand on n'est pas assez heureux pour le pouvoir faire, il faut se distraire, et surtout ne pas s'examiner de trop près." Too few introspectives have been afflicted with such scruples! Most of them seem to have indulged in self-probing with a gratification which amounts at times to delight.

The test is *sustained* introspection; and the enemy of sustained introspection is the day-dream. To this conclusion M. Jean Prévost is led by the resemblance between silent, prolonged introspection and states of mental feebleness. The end is laziness, "the laziness of indulgent reverie", he calls it, "the taste for continuing to dream when it prevents one getting out of bed". "Le journal est un oreiller de paresse..." wrote Amiel, late in life.

But there are subtler distractions than reverie.

Consider three notable writers who are introspective each in his way, Montaigne, Amiel and Proust, and compare the proportion of self-analysis in their work. One will find, I think, that while the amount of writing which is introspective in intention increases as one passes

LIMITS OF LITERARY INTROSPECTION 13

from the first to the later two, the tendency also increases to leave the narrow path of self-investigation, when it has once been found, and to run after images, under the impulse, perhaps, to resort to intuitive language where the rational fails. With the poet or the mystic this would be an appropriate exchange. But writers like the three we have chosen, involved in a more "scientific" attitude, are caught almost before they know it, as they exchange one medium for the other. Lured away from the self under the microscope, they lose themselves in vague ruminations or vaporous poetisings, the eye glued to the lens, the attention duped and distracted by the irrelevancies of their own fancy and phraseology. It was in order to tame the chimeras of his mind that Montaigne invented essay-writing. But Proust seems to have been the more keenly aware of the vice that waits at the end of the process. The *locus classicus* of its exposure is, I suggest, a passage to be found in *Albertine Disparue*, which must be quoted at length: "If, however, morning, noon and night, I never ceased to grieve over Albertine's departure, this did not mean that I was thinking only of her. For one thing, her charm having acquired a gradual ascendancy over things which, in course of time, were entirely detached from her, but were, nevertheless, electrified by the same emotion that she used to give me, if something made me think of Incarville or of the Verdurins, or of some new part that Lea was playing, a flood of suffering would overwhelm me. For another thing, what I myself called thinking of Albertine, was thinking of how I might bring her back, of how I might join her, might know what she was doing. With the result that if, during those hours of incessant martyrdom, there had been an illustrator present to represent the images which accompanied my sufferings, you would have seen pictures of the Gare d'Orsay, of the bank notes offered to Mme Bontemps, of St Loup stooping over the sloping desk of a telegraph office at which he was writing out a telegram for myself, never the picture of Albertine. Just as, throughout the whole course of our life, our egoism sees before it all the time the objects that are of interest to ourself, but never takes in that Ego itself which is incessantly observing them, so the desire which directs our actions descends towards them, but does not reascend to itself, whether because, being unduly utilitarian, it plunges into action and disdains knowledge, or because we have been looking to the future to compensate for the disappointments of the present, or because the inertia of our mind sends it sliding down the easy slope of imagination, rather than mounting up the steep slope of introspection. As a matter of fact, in those hours of crisis in which we would stake our whole life, in proportion as the person upon whom it depends reveals more clearly the immensity of the place that she occupies in our life, leaving nothing in the world which is not overthrown by her, so the image of that person diminishes until it is no longer perceptible. In everything we find the effect of her presence in the emotion that we feel; herself, the cause, we do not find anywhere."[1]

Proust shows us here something of the immense difficulty the mind experiences in trying to keep the object definitely in focus. Another kind of defect, differentiated

[1] Scott Moncrieff's translation: *The Sweet Cheat Gone*, pp. 67, 68. I have altered a few phrases.

by M. Prévost as "pseudo-introspection", must now claim our attention. "Most of those who think they are practising introspection", he says, "and offering a vast field to the inner eye deceive themselves greatly. All they do is to mimic the mental habits of other people or to allow the residuum of other people's thinking to combine at haphazard without adding to the mixture anything of their own" (p. 58).

Can Amiel be accused of so gross a form of self-deception? Casual speculation, stimulated by the books he was constantly reading or the conversations, discourses and sermons he listened to, is a major source of digression[1] or diversion in his Journal. The characteristic entries might be described as short, apt "essays" on general, objective topics, bearing the stamp of the writer's mind and art, but being anything but "fragments" of introspection. Conscious preoccupation with what is *objective* was one of this supremely personal diarist's most curious and contradictory traits. With him the relative intermittence of the introspective function may perhaps be explained by the conflicting urgency of what he calls his objective nature and interests. Early in life he wrote: "Je suis objectif and non subjectif", and he connected this with his tendency to receptivity, to absorption in, and identification with, the external— "de vivre de la vie universelle, et par conséquent de m'oublier moi-même". It was not till a quarter of a century later that he settled this problem for himself in the phrase: "Extrêmement subjectif par le sentiment et

[1] "Digression" from our standpoint, of course. Amiel's conception of the function of the journal varied greatly during the thirty or forty years he was preoccupied with keeping one. His earliest notions were certainly encyclopædic.

objectif par la pensée, ton individualité est d'être impersonnel et ton ennui de devoir être individuel" (II, pp. 160, 161).[1]

Finality of judgment in the case of Amiel must wait until the whole of his vast testament is published. With this reservation, we may consider his *Journal Intime* as an exception proving our rule. It is rich in introspective material, much of it free from the "digressions" and disabilities we have been noting, and marked by an inward tension sufficient at times to satisfy our exacting definition. Amiel is for us a master.[2] But while he has, among those we are considering, produced the largest *amount* of introspective writing, actually his mind works in a relatively narrow circle, revolving round the mystery of the self without being able to pierce it. Despite the variety of his interests, the immense programmes and promise of his beginnings, that asphyxiation he felt when reading the Journal of Maine de Biran may overcome those who progress through his. He knew how near he was to the same obsession.

But with this dolorous contraction, self-criticism gained an intensity, a candour all the more impressive. M. Jean Prévost seems to think that a little sincerity with themselves would show all introspective people that their inner thought, limited in its resources, fails almost always in its enterprises, silent meditation never reaching the end it has set itself. Without entering into the question of sincerity to oneself, he points out that what it admits and illuminates are passions and vices—

[1] *Fragments d'un Journal Intime*, ed. Bouvier.
[2] See the remarkable entry on the vocation of the diarist (I, p. 138).

elements of curiosity for the mind which discovers them in itself—but that it is almost always mute and hypocritical before the insufficiencies and platitudes of its own subjective method. The man who could come to doubt the clearness, the *depth* of his own interior vision would think himself dishonoured or would despair of his own mind (p. 79).

This surely goes too far. We have already seen one defect of method diagnosed by a modern introspective. In Amiel we find others. No one engaged in a similar task has been more conscious of, more desperately sincere about, the limits, defects and dangers of his method. During the later years, Amiel's Journal was largely devoted to its own apology. Among many shortcomings the diarist notes that the most penetrating of his intuitions, the most delicate of his intimate apperceptions, the most fugitive and precious of his thoughts are just those which he never registers (1, p. 111). One doubts, though, whether the reasons he gives for these omissions —"connaître me suffit trop: exprimer me semble parfois profaner"—really explain his disability.

The kind of "apology" to which we have just referred must not be confused with apology as a motive for autobiography. It is the excuse or explanation a man may give for keeping an account of his inner life. And it would have to be placed under what we have called "digressions", were it not capable of becoming one of the most direct means of illuminating the depths of the personality. We must be content to indicate a few of its dominant modes. The commonest is *preoccupation* with the intimate form—journal, "life" or essay—itself. This becomes a confidant with Maurice de Guérin and Amiel.

Or an obsession—and this obsession itself a source of qualms and scruples, but also of vitality, the very life of the man whose life it records—with Montaigne and again with Amiel. Then there is the *justification* of the intimate form, elaborated either to oneself (Amiel) or with the reader in view (Montaigne, in whom we shall find another apology than that for Raymond Sebond, viz. an intermittent apologetic for essay-writing). Allied to this is the effort to *define*, which frequently absorbed both Montaigne and Amiel. It may be noted, too, that Stendhal says some pertinent things on method and style in the first chapter of his autobiography; and that there is quite a display of explanation and exegesis in Barrès's trilogy, *Le culte du moi*. Rather than agree with M. Prévost on this head, I should prefer to generalise the remark made at Amiel's expense and to affirm that much literary introspection is preoccupied with its own examination and apology.

I shall refer later to Amiel's misguided preoccupation with general moralising. In this fault his predecessor, Sénancour, offends still more. French is a dangerous language to moralise in, because of the many examples it can show of the moralist at his best. "Tout est dit...", was the discouraging conclusion of one of the greatest of them, "Sur ce qui concerne les mœurs, le plus beau et le meilleur est enlevé; l'on ne fait que glaner après les anciens et les habiles d'entre les modernes." Amiel and Sénancour have neither the power nor the experience to vie with La Bruyère or with Vauvenargues, not to mention their predecessors. The particular and the personal are their specialities. The best they can do is to describe and analyse their own inner experiences. When

LIMITS OF LITERARY INTROSPECTION

they prescribe for the multitude, when they censure at large, one feels the amateur who has too readily persuaded himself that any man who can claim to know himself knows humanity. Sénancour made this claim with an almost pathetic faith in its validity for himself. Amiel is more cautious: "...tu n'as avancé qu'en un point, la connaissance de toi-même et (en gros) la connaissance de l'homme" (I, p. 138).

"In fact," said Sir Joshua Reynolds in one of his *Discourses*, "as he who does not know himself does not know others, so it may be said with equal truth that he who does not know others knows himself but imperfectly." This suggests the secret of the superiority of Montaigne. But first let us admit that Montaigne, in one of his best known utterances, seems to refute the point we have just made that the experience of some men is too narrow to allow them to moralise effectively. We have to show that, interpreted in the light of Montaigne's personal experience, there is no real contradiction to our thesis in the famous remark: "Je propose une vie basse et sans lustre, c'est tout un. On attache aussi bien toute la philosophie morale à une vie populaire et privée que à une vie de plus riche estoffe: chaque homme porte la forme entiere de l'humaine condition" (III, p. 27).[1]

First, we must discount Montaigne's modesty. It is his own life that he is proposing, and there have been lives more "low and lustreless" than his. We can acknowledge the wisdom of the remark that every man bears the complete form of humanity within him, and yet claim that men differ greatly in their conformity to

[1] *Essais*, ed. Villey.

anything that might be considered a human norm; still more do they differ in their ability to decipher the form within them. Montaigne's proposition seems to us to mean that favourable conditions, advantages and opportunities reveal nothing by themselves. Knowledge of life does not increase mechanically in direct ratio to richness of life. A humble and lustreless life lived to the full, intuitively experienced and intelligently interpreted, throws more light on the nature of existence than does just to have lived through a life of richer stuff. Experience, which is true living, is not quantitative: it is not a matter of accumulating "experiences", but of realising a relatively limited existence in a superior way.

Secondly, considering the rank universally given to Montaigne as an introspective writer, we shall attempt to show how surprisingly small is the *proportion* of introspective writing to be found in the Essays. The little volume of selections made by Émile Faguet for the *Temple Classics* would give a reader, unacquainted with the first twenty chapters of the original, an ill-balanced conception of the heterogeneous, contradictory and predominantly objective nature of Montaigne's interests. It is quality that tells again here; and the secret of Montaigne is, I think, that, capable as he is at times of the finest introspection, its fineness is due to the fact that, when he writes of himself, he writes of someone capable also of a high degree of "extraversion", having acquired, assimilated and stored much first-hand knowledge of the men, affairs and troublesome events of his time.

For the initial difficulty with introspection lies in the radical contradiction between the tension of inward awareness, its primary condition, and the demands of living, which must be largely external and concrete. With the majority of men development of the one is made at the expense, or to the exclusion, of the other. The instrument is perfected in a few rare cases, but the process brings no grist to the mill. Or the grist comes in abundance and there are no mill-stones to grind it. Few are the instances where favourable conditions of life, or superior endowments of intuition or wisdom at its disposal, have kept the balance and permitted the individual to mature in both directions at once or alternately. It is here perhaps that Montaigne is unique. His position is aptly defined in the words of another French precursor in the field we are now surveying: "He did not close his eyes to external life in its tumultuous incoherence; nor did he consider as negligible and unresourceful the great literary tradition of antiquity. But the knowledge of men bequeathed by books, the experience of the men with whom he had mingled—all this, with ever more deliberate premeditation, he made to serve the elaboration of his own being; not narrowing it down to the measure of himself, but bringing it to the test of his consciousness—broadening his range so as to comprehend everything, and nourishing his inner life both on the deepest things that human life could teach him about his own powers and weaknesses, as well as on the fine and useful things which he derived from all kinds of wisdom."[1]

[1] Joachim Merlant, *De Montaigne à Vauvenargues*, Paris, 1914.

CHAPTER II

MONTAIGNE'S SELF-PORTRAITURE AND THE DEFINITION OF THE ESSAYS

I

SINCE Brunetière French scholarship has renewed and illuminated the study of the Essays by treating them as products of a development in the mind and manner of Montaigne. They are now presented as a progressive experiment in a new personal mode, approaching perfection of type as the impulse to self-expression realises itself more clearly and more masterfully. To concentrate on the autobiographical aspect and to attempt to unravel its development seems therefore to involve that difficult but alluring issue, the definition of the Essays. Conversely, to note how Montaigne defines his impulse or intention at different stages of the work in progress should throw light, not only on the nature of the Essays, but through them on the author. Actually, as we shall see, Montaigne's explanation of the task in hand and his deepest self-revelations synchronise with a regularity which, though not absolute, suggests something more fundamental than coincidence. What introspection is revealed in the Essays seems to me to stand in close relation to apology. But first let us inquire into the nature of autobiography in them.

It would be unprofitable to discuss this question without reference to the views of Pierre Villey, whose death

MONTAIGNE'S SELF-PORTRAITURE 23

in 1934 deprived France of one of her greatest workers on the sixteenth-century background.[1] In the strict sense, as Villey pointed out, the term "autobiography" is not applicable. The Essays are not the journal of a sequence of events or experiences. They do not represent the chronology of a life, though they show on investigation an extremely interesting evolution. "La peinture du moi", the portraiture of the self, is the phrase Villey adopts for referring to this aspect of the Essays, or rather to Montaigne's essential preoccupation and activity in writing them; and the phrase is authentic. It is, with some significant variations, the Essayist's way of describing what he was doing. And it was by insisting on the "charmant projet de se peindre" that Voltaire reset the balance in his favour after Pascal had disturbed it by denouncing the "moi" as "haïssable".

But what did Montaigne mean by the "peinture du moi"? His *Avis au lecteur*, that most ingratiating of introductions, seems to answer this very question, and to present all that follows, without discrimination, as fulfilling the definition. Yet if the Essays are read in chronological order,[2] the second book will have been reached before one is found in which the author is clearly painting his own portrait. It should be noticed, however, that the eighth chapter of Book I, *De l'Oisiveté*, is at once the first personal essay and the earliest account which Montaigne gives of how he began to write. His retirement to the tower of his country house, which preceded the experiment by about a year (1571), had

[1] See especially *Les Sources et l'Évolution des Essais de Montaigne*, 2nd edition, Paris, 1933, vol. II.
[2] Recent editions tend to facilitate this. References here are to Pierre Villey's edition in three volumes, Paris, Alcan, 1922–1923.

revealed his mind possessed by a swarm of "chimeres et monstres fantasques" which he felt constrained to pin down in writing, hoping, as he says, to make them ashamed of themselves and so reduce his thoughts to order. With this exception the first chapters in their earliest form (1580) were almost exclusively taken up with the deeds and thoughts of other men—modern instances, ancient "curiosités", any topic however "vain". What they resemble most are the centos or compilations popular at a time when the anthologising mania of the humanists was still at its height. This compiler's habit Montaigne never quite threw off. For modern readers it can trouble the enjoyment of some of the best chapters. Before 1580, however, its domination was past and Montaigne was capable of elaborating a theme in a manner as profoundly personal as that of the most mature parts of his work. This change in method owed much, it appears, to the discovery of Plutarch—especially of the Opuscules—in Amyot's translation. A more intimate cause is traced to the first attacks (1578) of the malady which was to prove fatal fourteen years later.

The process of self-portraiture seems to have begun around the year 1579. Montaigne's professed wish at that time was to leave his friends and relatives a memorial of himself. The *Avis au lecteur*, which must have been written just as the first two books were going to press, gracefully woos the disinterested reader by advising him not to open a book destined for the author's kith and kin. We find the process well illustrated in the tenth, seventeenth and eighteenth chapters of the second book and in the beginning of chapter thirty-seven.

Let us glance at II, x. Its title is *Des Livres*. The distinction between erudition, the approach of the scholar, and reading for pleasure, that of an "ignorant" man like the author, runs throughout. Actually the subject is Montaigne—"Ce sont icy mes fantasies, par lesquelles je ne tasche point à donner à connoistre les choses, mais moy"—or rather Montaigne as a reader and judge of books. He talks almost exclusively of his tastes and preferences, sprinkling some great criticism with "asides" on his habits and humours as a browser and borrower from books.

We find the purest self-portraiture in II. xviii Except for an interpolated passage to be mentioned later, the "Avis au lecteur" mood dominates here as it did in the previous case. The argument is an apology for writing about oneself, which is justifiable only in the case of a great man. Montaigne, however, is not making a public statue but a bust for a library. What a pleasure it would be for him to hear someone describe, as he does, the ways, aspect, expression, common speech and fortunes of his ancestors! It would reveal an evil nature, he thinks, to despise the portraits of our friends and predecessors, the shape of their clothes and of their arms.

It is obvious that the art of self-portraiture, as practised so far by the Essayist, has little or nothing to do with introspection. The twentieth chapter of the same book is another that is richly personal, but which yields the same result on inspection. Of the nineteen which follow, the last alone is personal. And of this, *De la Ressemblance des Enfans aux Peres*, the first fifth contributes a description of Montaigne's malady to the "peinture du moi"; the rest deals with medicine and doctors and the writer's antipathy to them.

Deliberate self-portraiture is then most characteristic of one phase in particular of the Essays, and is best exemplified in the personal chapters of the second book. Even there most of what Montaigne says of himself is descriptive and external, and much has not escaped the verdict of triviality. Later on, in the third book (1588)—"ce troisiesme alongeail du reste des pieces de ma peinture" (III, p. 240)—the study of the self is universalised on the basis that "chaque homme porte la forme entiere de l'humaine condition" (III, p. 27). The project or design has by now expanded into a study of mankind through the medium of the self. The originality of the last book lies, as Villey admitted, in "l'expression d'une pensée philosophique dans le Moi et par le Moi de Montaigne". The much worked phrase cannot therefore have had a constant and invariable meaning for the author. Used first in its literal sense, after an early phase of objective experimentation, it must have become for him, as his method and interests broadened, a convenient and elastic metaphor. As it is now considered legitimate to qualify the definition offered by Montaigne in the *Avis au lecteur* and to limit its scope, the question suggests itself whether the grounds for proposing literary self-portraiture as the master key to the definition of his work are sufficiently strong to justify its acceptance as a complete explanation of the origin and purpose of the Essays.

II

This does not dispose of the whole of the personal side. There are many references to the self which fall outside the strict interpretation we have given to the "peinture du moi". Having followed the chronological method of approach, we have so far taken the Essays in their primitive form. The edition of 1580 was amplified in 1588, and from then annotated by the author until his death in 1592. Most of these additions are increasingly personal in character. Villey called them "additions-confidences".

They seem to conform to two categories. Some are examples or illustrations drawn from Montaigne's behaviour or experience, and then they do not differ from the previous instances except in having been inserted *explicitly* as illustrations. Others are passages, more curious and interesting than the former, in which Montaigne discusses what might be called his "introspective method".

A good specimen of the first type will be found in I, xiv. The writer has reached the conclusion that it is not dearth but abundance which produces avarice. The passage that follows (mostly B)[1] takes up a third of the chapter in its final form, and begins: "Je veux dire mon experience autour de ce subject." His experience is given in three phases ("trois sortes de condition"), exemplifying his attitudes at different stages of life to the question of money and his habits in respect of saving and spending. The result is a concrete illustration of the main theme drawn from the life of the writer. In no sense introspective, it is personal but not even intimate. One is tempted to ask whether the deliberate portraiture of the self does not serve the same purpose as these

[1] (B) represents additions and interpolations which first appeared in the edition of 1588, (C) represents all those of a later date.

illustrations, but on a larger scale, the essay-portraits being simply more fully developed *examples* casually introduced into the natural sequence of the chapters. One would, if that were conceded, have to allow that self-portraiture often got the better of the Essayist, who could indulge in it, when the mood was favourable, with a relish which he excused as memoir-writing for his descendants. But this would merely bring out the whimsical inconsistency of the Essays which conform to no scheme or plan—though there may be a more persistent motive behind them than the portraiture of the author.[1]

We have claimed that most of the interpolated personal references are there as illustrations; we have now to admit that *some* require a different explanation. As one advances over the chequered surface of the Essays in their final form, one comes increasingly upon brief intrusions or eruptions from a deeper plane—alluring figures and images which have a marked introspective flavour, as when Montaigne says of himself: "Comme celuy qui continuellement me couve de mes pensées, et les couche en moy, je suis à tout' heure preparé environ ce que je puis estre" (I, pp. 109, 110). The (C) passage, which forms the last third of II, vi, contains perhaps the most remarkable of all these "introspective" images— one which Brunetière commented on: "...de penetrer les profondeurs opaques de ses replis internes." This addition should be read through; it is unfortunately too

---

[1] Villey's view was that "les jugements de Montaigne font partie de la peinture de ses mœurs et de sa vie" (*Les Essais de Michel de Montaigne*, in the series, "Les Grands Événements littéraires", p. 8). I should make *judgment* the inclusive term. See Chapter III.

AND THE DEFINITION OF THE ESSAYS 29

long to be included here. In it a profound conception of the study of the self is brilliantly adumbrated. But that it is an interpolation must have been clear without the editor's indication. The passage has a tension, a density not frequent in Montaigne, who attains to introspective concentration no more easily than any of the great introspectives. "Ce ne sont mes gestes que j'escris, c'est moy, c'est mon essence", is an affirmation which, taken literally, is compatible in tone and implication with only a few sections of the Essays. Other passages comparable to this one are more fragmentary in texture and less sustained.[1] They suggest that the feeling Montaigne had of his introspective powers was deeper than any actual achievement of his in direct self-investigation could show. Was he groping after still more intense probings and illuminations of the self, which he did not live to prosecute, and of which these phrases are but scattered premonitions? Here, in Florio's translation, is a suggestion that he was: "When I have gone as far as I can, I have no whit pleased myself: for the further I saile the more land I descry, and that so dimmed with fogges and overcast with clouds, that my sight is weakened, I cannot distinguish the same." (Cf. Villey, I, p. 188.)

This question involves another. How far was the introspective habit really germane to Montaigne's type of mind? M. André Gide made an interesting remark and indicated a pertinent quotation in the course of his *Essai sur Montaigne* (1929). Of the author of the Essays

[1] Cf. II, xvii, the (A) passage beginning "Or mes opinions..." (pp. 443, etc.), and II, xviii, the (C) passage beginning 'Et quand personne ne me lira..." (pp. 452, etc.).

he said: "Très différent d'Amiel, et en général de tous les 'analystes', il écrit fort judicieusement: Cecy m'advient aussi, que je ne me trouve où je me cherche et me trouve plus par rencontre que par l'inquisition de mon jugement" (I, p. 47). We must agree, in any systematic sense Montaigne is not an introspective. His self-revelations are sporadic intuitions rather than conscious pieces of self-analysis. This is clear even from the long passage referred to, in which the deeper phrases strike upward, as it were, through the crust of a discussion of method.

There is yet another point to consider. The passage in question is appended to the famous description of a fall from horseback, with the lesson which Montaigne drew from this experience. The appendage begins: "Et ne me doibt on sçavoir mauvais gré pour tant, si je la communique. Ce qui me sert, peut aussi par accident servir à un autre. Au demeurant, je ne gaste rien, je n'use que du mien. Et, si je fay le fol, c'est à mes despends et sans l'interest de personne. Car c'est en follie qui meurt en moy, qui n'a point de suitte" (II, vi, 64). The argument, it will be seen, while it explicates his method, is a *defence* of that method, an apology for the "peinture du moi" in its most intimate sense. What has happened, apparently, in the "evolution" of the Essays is this, that personal references and illustrations have gradually supplanted the former type of example drawn from history, ancient and contemporary literature, superstition and fable, and that now and then they are given full rein, sometimes to the extent of a whole essay. It is then that the author feels the exceptionalness of his work: "C'est le seul livre au monde de son espece,

AND THE DEFINITION OF THE ESSAYS 31

d'un dessein farouche et extravagant" (II, viii). If, as I think, the deepest introspective *aperçus* occur just when Montaigne is concerned to explain and defend his design, one is brought back to the definition of the Essays. The sentence immediately following the one given above (II, vi) runs thus: "Nous n'avons nouvelles que de deux ou trois anciens qui ayent battu ce chemin; et si ne pouvons dire si c'est du tout en pareille maniere à cette-cy, n'en connoissant que les noms. Nul depuis ne s'est jetté sur leur trace." The problem of the genre is obviously in Montaigne's mind, and the passage proceeds with the description of his "thorny enterprise". At this point I am tempted to indulge in a speculation which will not, I hope, seem entirely fantastic.

I suggest that most of the deeply personal things in the Essays are involved in the excuses of a gentleman who is conscious of having talked often and at length about himself. The first aim that formed in his mind, as issues became clearer and his experiment took shape, was, not as yet to paint his own portrait, still less to seek in himself the "forme entiere de l'humaine condition". Montaigne simply found himself drawn, but with increasing magnetism, to the discussion of moral and philosophical topics—matters of wisdom (the wisdom of this world), and affairs public and private. The taste for exercising his judgment on these things grows as he ponders them until the function absorbs him. His purpose is now to discuss them freely and *à fond*. By "à fond" I do not mean "thoroughly" (otherwise Montaigne would have written treatises), but by "essaying", when it pleases him, the most searching or subversive, the most daringly indiscreet, the most disconcertingly true things he happens to think or feel. To do this he must refer to himself—"mon theme se renverse en soy" (III, p. 386)—and these references produce the most intimate disclosures, and require further apologies and qualifications. The Essays do contain startling revelations for a man to make about himself. Only rarely is the confession "scandalous"—not as often, Montaigne pretends, as he could have wished. Their audacity appears more in the extremes to which he will push any train of thought that appeals to him at the moment—we may remember that the work was ultimately put on the Index—and still more in the trivial, belittling, gratuitous nature of what he sometimes records. For as Rousseau was later to insist: "Ce n'est pas ce qui est criminel qui coûte le plus à dire, c'est ce qui est ridicule et honteux." This is largely what gives Montaigne the feeling of his own novelty, the sense he has of the strangeness and riskiness of his design. He knew he would be criticised for it, but he persists. Yet he is cautious as well as "cauteleux": the half-indulgent, self-reproachful tone creeps in whenever he refers to his own outspokenness. One day or another, or perhaps gradually, the originality of what he was doing, the unprecedented egotism of the Essays comes home to their author, and he makes this the explanation of, and the excuse for, the whole experiment. Yes, it was self-portraiture he had in mind from the first: "Ainsi, lecteur, je suis moy-mesmes la matiere de mon livre...."

But we should guard against concluding from any single statement or phrase of his, however final or full of conviction it may sound, that we have here indubitably the key to the mystery of his work. M. Gide has said that if all the passages in which Montaigne speaks of himself were suppressed, the bulk would be reduced by a third—the best third. Even at this estimate the major portion falls outside the category of direct subjective expression. And if we admit that what is not subjectively expressed may yet be personal and original to a supreme degree, we should still contend that to apply the phrase, "peinture du moi", to writing which is personal in so broad a sense is to deprive it of precise meaning. It is probably futile to attempt to reduce the Essays to a norm, a type, a definition, yet at this fascinating game we shall not be the last to lose our stakes. We may also be sure that whatever conclusion our inquiry has led us to adopt, somewhere in their "replis internes" there lurks a gracious but categorical refutation. We are left with the hope not to be the first to incur a visit from that other world, whence their author promised to return to those who have misrepresented him, even though their intention was to do him honour.

CHAPTER III

JUDGMENT AND RELATION IN THE ESSAYS OF MONTAIGNE

BY their complexities and contradictions the Essays of Montaigne seem to invite an endless variety of interpretations. For their elucidation the search of some principle of unity is both a necessity and a peril. The difficulty of relying on the "peinture du moi" is that it cannot open all the doors of the mystery of the design. Not only does it leave most of the first book unexplained, it cannot even be applied to the majority of Essays in the second; while in the third, self-portraiture is subsumed under a larger issue. This conclusion appears inevitable when we keep the phrase strictly to its literal meaning. The more elastic use Pierre Villey made of it ends in vagueness through the number of modifications to which it becomes liable; and Villey himself saw the danger.[1] Is there not a more reliable common denominator which will help us to avoid the conclusion that the problem of definition is ultimately insoluble?

Another line of investigation has suggested itself. What meaning did Montaigne attach to the name he gave to his original genre? In what sense did he use the word "essai"? According to Villey the word was employed probably for the first time as a generic term in the fiftieth chapter of Book I. If so, all essays in the

[1] Cf. *Les Sources*, etc. II, pp. 277–279.

literary sense owe their christening to this phrase: "Le jugement est un util à tous subjects, et se mesle par tout. A cette cause, aux essais que j'en fay ici, j'y employe toute sorte d'occasion. Si c'est un subject que je n'entende point, à cela mesme je l'essaye, sondant le gué de bien loing..." (I, p. 383).

We notice that here Montaigne conceives of the judgment as infinitely applicable, and of his Essays as the trials of his judgment. Let us then take "judgment" as our key-word. With the reservation already made about the danger of entrusting the explanation of the genre to a single term, I suggest that, better than any other, the word "judgment" will fit all varieties of the Essays. "Le jugement tient chez moy un siege magistral", wrote Montaigne in the last of them. But from the beginning he was preoccupied with how to judge men, and he was already conscious of difficulty: "Certes, c'est un subject merveilleusement vain, divers, et ondoyant, que l'homme. Il est malaisé d'y fonder jugement constant et uniforme" (I, p. 8). In the course of Book I we can detect him working out a method, occupied in turn, though never systematically, with three aspects of the training of judgment. First, the perfecting of his own as an instrument—its "assouplissement", to use Villey's word—and also its strengthening and enlightenment: "Je veux icy entasser aucunes façons anciennes que j'ay en memoire, les unes de mesme les nostres, les autres differentes, afin qu'ayant en l'imagination cette continuelle variation des choses humaines, nous en ayons le jugement plus esclaircy et plus ferme" (I, p. 378). Secondly, the training of judgment in the young through an education concentrating mainly on this aim at the expense of memory training (I, xxv and xxvi). Thirdly, the training of judgment in view of a favourite, though never an exclusive, end. Judgment must be given the widest grounds for exercise, from the most trivial daily acts to the finer matters of taste; but of supreme importance is its application to moral issues, ranging from the recognition of the highest good down to the estimate of a common custom, a particular habit or an individual mode of conduct. In the apt phrase, Montaigne excels in the "jugement de mœurs"; his Essays are "l'estude que je traitte de nos mœurs et mouvemens" (I, p. 133).

This is not, we admit, the first time that Montaigne's definition (or one of his many definitions) has been taken literally. But the view here proposed is that the Essays are essentially concerned with the observation of men (and of the author) *in relation to moral action and interaction*, and with the judgment applied not dogmatically but experimentally to such inclinations. Montaigne, it should be noticed, is not interested in actions as such, concrete or physical, apart from their significance. He denies that his own are worth recording. Fortune puts them on too low a level; what he registers are his opinions (II, p. 216). But he also wrote: "Toute action est propre à nous faire connoistre" (I, p. 384, note 3), or as it appeared later: "Tout mouvement nous descouvre"; and there is no contradiction. Action for Montaigne is the gesture that reveals motive or impulse. It is the sign of being alive, of being oneself. Action is being: "D'autant que nous avons cher, estre; et estre consiste en mouvement et action" (II, p. 76).

This activist attitude to psychology reveals a French

moralist of the great line. The mind—the "will" Croce called it—in deliberation for action; the perplexities presented by alternatives of action; the meditation which analyses or the dispute which exposes the motives and consequences of action—such is the stuff of the tragedies of Corneille and Racine. After Ronsard, and in a psychological sense, Montaigne may be called the first classicist in French literature. This explains why he is not introspective in the passive, post-classical manner. It is with the appraisement of the self in adventurous or apprehensive movement that he is concerned, not with the scrutiny of the self immobilised in dejection. The superiority of his revelation is its concern with a man very much alive, not with the semi-atrophied being that Amiel watched stiffening under the microscope. Both give us death scenes. Amiel annotates his decline poignantly: "Nuit terrible. Azrael a passé sur moi à trois heures du matin...." Montaigne described the "death" from which he recovered as a lesson which taught him to master the fear of death.

Montaigne's interest in the self is therefore an interest in its moral and social *rapports*—never a purely scientific or "psychological" investigation, never pure or purposeless introspection. Montaigne is attracted to the problem of the individual, but of the individual living and active in society, never to the life of the solitary. Personal religion, it will be remembered, is conspicuously absent from his considerations; though he fully appreciates the social advantage of a "State Church". This interest, with its moral bias, is a rival motif to the self-explanatory moods and their consequences noticed previously. Usually it occurs in the form of a recommendation of self-examination as a means to self-improvement, or as the initial stage in a proper realisation or adaptation of the self. There are thus two types of introspection discernible in the Essays. The one occurs when the author attempts to define (and defend) the Essays as the expression of the self of the writer; the other, when he applies his judgment to himself in view of correction or improvement. This type of self-examination never reaches the depth of introspection to which the former sometimes attains.

The supreme estimate of the moral advantages of self-knowledge is the chapter on *Experience*, which is the last of the series. As a pendant to the more purely introspective passages referred to above, I suggest, as one of the best examples of Montaigne's evaluation of self-knowledge, and as the moral justification of the Essays, that section of III, xiii which begins with the phrase: "Je m'estudie plus qu'autre subject. C'est ma metaphisique, c'est ma phisique" (p. 390). Starting from the position that whatever profit we draw from experience, that of others will instruct us little if we can derive none from our own, it closes with the nonchalant but significant remark: "Enfin, toute cette fricassée que je barbouille icy n'est qu'un registre des essais ('expériences', Villey) de ma vie...", and he suggests that for the health of one's soul it might be well to reverse the lesson.

Montaigne, we may be sure, did not mean his example to be neglected. In the ninth chapter of Book III, he speaks of the Essays as "la publication de mes mœurs". He refers in the same place to the malevolence and "sickness" of contemporary judgments. The times are out of joint and, as he says elsewhere, "Nos jugements sont encore malades et suivent la depravation de nos mœurs."

In pursuing his experimental ruminations on the nature of the moral judgment, how far was the author of the Essays deliberately reacting against the ruthless irrationality, the notorious intolerance and injustice of his time? The answer to this question might prove conclusively that Montaigne was the opposite of the "introspective type"—a man who, having corrected the intimate warring of his members, had trained them to attain that equilibrium of powers which makes for harmony, liberty and service, and who could present the result as a direct example to his fellows. This would justify even his extravagances: "Dieu veuille que cet excès de ma licence attire nos hommes jusques à la liberté" (III, p. 82). It would also endorse one of the earliest appreciations of Montaigne, that of La Croix du Maine, who praised him in particular for his "emerveillable jugement".

An answer to such a question was given over a dozen years ago by the late Dr A. Armaingaud, doyen of Montaigne enthusiasts and scholars. Brought up on the Essays from the age of seven, he completed a devotion of nearly seventy years by editing the entire works for the publisher, Louis Conard (Paris, 1924). The long study which serves as introduction offers a thesis which is of interest to us, though it should not be accepted without reservation.

Dr Armaingaud presents us with what I venture to call an "extraverted" or externalised Montaigne. His introduction deliberately ignores the study of the self.

"Montaigne", he says, "is too exclusively represented as a writer whose principal object was to paint the self; he is far from having done so completely, either because, contrary to common opinion, he was too modest, or rather because he wrote for other reasons..." (p. 2). His emphasis of the public side of the Essayist's life and thought makes one feel as if the semi-retirement of Montaigne to his "librairie" has been exaggerated into something like the withdrawal of a Romantic into his *tour d'ivoire*. Michel de Montaigne had political preoccupations, practical aspirations for the good of his country, which centred in Henry of Navarre. From 1574 to 1587 he was actively interested in the fortunes of the Béarnais, whom he was able, before his death, to salute as Henry IV of France. Most of the Essays were composed during this period. Far from being the meditations of a solitary, they were the work of a man who, as Mayor of Bordeaux, could write, in a letter to Marshal de Matignon: "J'ai passé toutes les nuits, ou par la ville en armes, ou hors de la ville sur le port...." They are thus "un livre d'action et de combat" (*Étude*, p. 205). And, as the cause of Henry of Navarre was involved in that of religious liberty, his book is still more "un livre de combat pour la tolérance" (p. 221). The Essays helped to prepare opinion for the Edict of Nantes. The venture depended largely on the method of presentation. By his captivating style, his preference for gentle exhortation rather than the *ex professo* manner, Montaigne succeeded in being what every other publicist of his time failed to be—a universal "enchanteur", acceptable to both sides.

This may be true of Montaigne; but before we accept

it as true of the Essays we should think it over in the light of Brunetière's remark: "There is a whole public life to Montaigne's account to which we hardly find a reference in the Essays except incidentally. Moreover, he has scarcely mentioned the events of his time."[1] Yet it is not possible to deny that they reverberate with recommendations to moderation, and that no lesson was needed more when they appeared. The tone of "gentle exhortation" is unmistakable. To admit even this points to the *sense of relation* between author and reader which removes the Essays by a whole heaven from that asphyxiating atmosphere of self-centredness which has been found characteristic of at least one *Journal Intime*. In contradistinction to other explorers of the ego, Montaigne was one who, as we have tried to show, thought and wrote with a social implication, even when concentrating upon himself: "Cette longue attention que j'employe à me considerer me dresse à juger aussi passablement des autres, et est peu de choses dequoy je parle plus heureusement et excusablement" (III, xiii).

[1] *Histoire de la Littérature française classique*, I, p. 619.

CHAPTER IV

THE INNER LIFE OF A PHILOSOPHER: MAINE DE BIRAN'S *JOURNAL INTIME*

I

"NOTHING is so melancholy and wearisome as this Journal of Maine de Biran. This unchanging monotony of perpetual reflection has an enervating and a depressing effect upon one. Here, then, is the life of a distinguished man seen in its most intimate aspects! It is one long repetition, in which the only change is an almost imperceptible displacement of centre in the writer's manner of viewing himself." So wrote H. F. Amiel in his Journal on the 18th June 1857, in the course of reading Ernest Naville's book on Maine de Biran.[1] One wonders how far the severities and superficialities of his conclusions might have been modified by acquaintance with the fuller record recently edited by M. de la Valette-Monbrun.[2] Even this edition is not complete. It is composed of dated and undated fragments, gaps in the Journal being filled so far as possible by extracts from a pocket-book, often mere notes of appointments and affairs. The original is missing for the years 1797–1814, owing, it is intimated, to the negligence of those who had charge of the personal papers left at the death of the philosopher.

[1] Ernest Naville, *Maine de Biran, sa vie et ses pensées*, Geneva, 1851; Paris, 1857 and 1874.
[2] *Journal Intime de Maine de Biran*, publié par A. de la Valette-Monbrun, Paris, Plon, vol. I, 1927, vol. II, 1931.

In a note to the first fragment the editor explains that the entries for the early years are concerned far more with the philosopher's ideas than with himself. The second volume, representing the last eight years of his life, is full of intimate items showing an acute apperception of some of the deepest problems of the soul. But the Journal as a whole is very far from having the variety of Amiel's. It runs to thirteen hundred pages, while the manuscript left by the Swiss diarist is said to reach nearly seventeen thousand. The "confessions" of each of these descendants of Rousseau show characteristic alternations of interest, as between a concentration on the ego, coloured with self-recrimination, and an expansive delight in natural scenery. Amiel had travelled more widely and was doubtless the more varied reader of the two. He is conscious both of his similarities to, and of his superiorities over, his predecessor. "In this eternal self-chronicler and observer", he wrote on the day before entering the remarks from which we have quoted, "I seem to see myself reflected with all my faults—indecision, discouragement, over-dependence on sympathy, difficulty of finishing—with my habits of watching myself feel and live, with my growing incapacity for practical action, with my aptitude for psychological study. But I have also discovered some differences which cheer and console me. This nature is, as it were, only one of the men who exist in me! It is one of my departments. It is not the whole of my territory, the whole of my inner kingdom. Intellectually, I am more objective and more constructive; my horizon is vaster; I have seen much more of men, things, countries, peoples, and books; I have a greater mass of

44   THE INNER LIFE OF A PHILOSOPHER:

experiences—in a word, I feel that I have more culture, greater wealth, range, and freedom of mind, in spite of my wants, my limits, and my weaknesses...."

Amiel was sincere in making the comparison turn in his favour. In some points, however, he must have been mistaken. "Intellectually more objective and more constructive"—yet Maine de Biran ranks high as a philosopher while Amiel is remembered only as the author of a very subjective diary. "A greater mass of experiences"—chiefly bookish experiences, one suspects. Amiel's existence has nothing to show comparable to the relatively varied activities of Maine de Biran.

Born at Bergerac in 1766 and educated by the Pères Doctrinaires of Périgueux, the young man entered the life-guards under Louis XVI and was present at Versailles on the memorable days of October 1789. The horrors of the Revolution he escaped by withdrawing to Grateloup, a property near his birthplace. Here, as he said, he passed *per saltum* from frivolity to philosophy.

After the Restoration he held the offices of treasurer to the Chamber of Deputies and member of the Council of State. During the Autumn recesses he would return to his country home to pursue his studies, lamenting the enforced journeys by coach from the beneficent quiet of Périgord to the distractions of the capital. Through a sense of duty, not by choice or vocation, the philosopher had become a man of affairs. Embarrassed by ill-health, timidity and self-consciousness, he played a minor but persistent role in the intellectual life and society of Paris; his associates counted among the most celebrated thinkers, the most prominent political and social leaders of the period.

Maine de Biran died in 1824. Few of his works had been published during his lifetime; and it was not until 1859, when Ernest Naville brought out the three volumes of *Œuvres inédites*, that a connected view of his philosophical development was possible. In origin it goes back to Condillac, but the sensationalist basis was gradually abandoned on the strength of a conviction that the method of the Idéologues was inadequate to the problem they set out to solve. Biran follows de Tracy in stressing the importance of movement; but he goes further, making the power of movement, as distinct from the faculty of feeling, the basis of his new position. Distinguishing sense impressions as those which are passive (sensations) and those which are active (perceptions), he claimed that it is the voluntary effort involved in the latter which gives a sense of the self. Resistance and effort are the sources of knowledge, including self-knowledge. The irreducible proof of the ego is found in the inner conviction of volition; and the establishment of a real identity between motor effort, the will and the self is the original contribution of this view.

Biran does not appear to have remained faithful for long to the type of education he had received from the Doctrinaires of Périgueux. While he was in touch with the Idéologues he seems to have shared their prejudices against religion. Nor was he nearer to religion when engaged on his doctrine of effort. Morally at that time he was a stoic. But certain spiritual preoccupations were, if not awakened, revived by the events of 1814 and the anxieties into which an aristocrat who had served the Restoration was plunged by Napoleon's return. Thrown back on the ego Maine de Biran is now unable to find in himself a support against the instabilities of his life. From now on he seeks God, the Christian God, impelled not by dialectical argument but by a need of the soul. The Journal he left is the confidant of the manifold vicissitudes through which this search was made. The works themselves, finished or unfinished, have of recent years been acknowledged with increasing respect as the foundation of modern spiritualistic philosophy, constituted as a doctrine of the consciousness which neglects neither the infra- nor the supra-conscious influences to which the ego is related.

Maine de Biran's critic, the disheartened professor of aesthetics, could cite no such distractions as his excuse and was engaged on no comparable achievement. In the end he had nothing left to live for but his Journal, that is, in the narrowest sense, himself. For, as Montaigne said of the Essays, he no more made his book than his book made him. By exhaustive elimination of all external ties, by the gradual atrophy of his numerous antennae, Amiel becomes *the* Introspective, searching more deeply, more curiously and persistently perhaps than anyone unaided by a modern technique has searched into the narrowing, desiccated pit of the self. Biran rivals him here, but he is less "pure" in motive. His introspection acquires a more or less conscious trend which is absent from the stagnant heart-searchings of Amiel. With time it becomes purposeful, ultimately aspiring beyond and above the self. And it was always less out of touch with externals, less "asphyxiating" than the Swiss diarist could have perceived. From this angle we should place Maine de Biran somewhere between Amiel and (with reservations) Montaigne.

"J'ai aussi mes *Essais* à faire", he writes; yet his ideal is far removed from that of the Essays, as he understands them. "Our amour-propre", he says, "always carries us outward, as far from ourselves as possible to save us from feeling our misery and seeing ourselves as we are. Yet nothing is more necessary to our life, present and future,... than this inner life, the confessions of weakness and affection that a soul makes to itself and to other souls capable of understanding it. This is how human nature can be better known. Montaigne did not paint himself or confess himself in this sense. He was not a mild and sensitive soul, humble and sincere, ready to confess, reveal and express himself as he feels at bottom; he was a mind full of artificial riches and ideas of all kinds, some his own, some acquired, displaying itself in leisurely, cavalier fashion, laying aside all customary formalities, so that he can speak of himself and of all things just as he thinks" (II, p. 310).

Maine de Biran conforms to the type which he implies is opposed to Montaigne: "I am the most personal man that one could find, and I have always been so. There is an instinct which forces me irresistibly to exist in myself, to concern myself with all that touches me closely in the material or intellectual spheres" (II, p. 207). He goes like a somnambulist through the world of affairs, having, in Le Roy's phrase, the "vocation d'intériorité". None could surpass the philosopher himself in defining and delimiting his function: "I neglect expressions, I never make phrases in my head, I study, I investigate ideas for their own sake, to know them as they are, for what they contain; and I do so with the utmost disinterest, free from passion and amour-propre. Such a disposition fits me for psychological research and the inner life, but removes me from all the rest. I have also frequented men enough to know them, and in all their external habits I read what they are and what are the motives behind them. I watch them act without acting myself" (II, p. 7).

The man who could make these claims was an introspective philosopher, a natural psychologist above everything else. Of this his personal conception of the new science adds a further proof: "In psychology observation is but meditation. What is opposed everywhere else is completely identified here. It is a question of finding, recognising one's object, and one only finds it within, that is by meditation" (II, p. 318). He shows at times a sense of the depths of the problem comparable to that of the investigators of the Unconscious. Lacking their method, he has to rely on his own resources. "The *inner man* is ineffable in his essence; how many degrees of profundity, how many aspects of the inner man have not yet even been glimpsed but may be ultimately, for one point of view leads to another. A person who can meditate, who advances to a certain point in this inward intuition, gives others the means of going still further..." (II, p. 193).

It is natural that for such a thinker every psychological system in which one leaves out the *conscium*, the inner apperception of the self, should be nothing but physics or logic (II, p. 251). There is no true psychology save that of the inner man: "I can understand how the inner light is ignored," he writes, "when one aspires only to found systems; but when one wants truth before everything else, it must be sought where it is: at the source nearest and most intimate to ourselves. How, moreover, can one avoid being brought back ceaselessly to the *great mystery of one's own existence* by the astonishment it causes to any thinking being! I myself felt this astonishment early in life. The spontaneous and continual changes which I have never ceased to feel, which I still feel every day, have prolonged that surprise and hardly allow me to be seriously occupied with extraneous things or with things having no relation to this ever present phenomenon, *this enigma that I bear within me always*, to which I never find the key, because whenever I think I have seized it under one aspect it appears under another" (II, p. 309).

II

We have traced so far the development of a conception of philosophy (psychology) proceeding from the realisation of an inner vocation and the conscious possession of a mature though native method of self-scrutiny. But this is to start in the middle of a process. Maine de Biran has recorded what he considers to be the origination of his habit of introspection. He is persuaded that he owes what he is to a defective physique: "When one has little life in one, or a feeble sense of life, one is the more inclined to observe interior phenomena. This is what made me a psychologist so early" (II, p. 162).

Of great importance in the growth of this thinker's mind is the painfully persistent realisation of the variability of the self under changes of climate and physical mood. "No man, perhaps," he writes, "has been organised as I have been to recognise the subordination of the moral to a given physical state. The brusque variations through which all my faculties pass successively are certainly quite spontaneous, and all that is spontaneous is organic and mechanical, even though they be the *élans* of genius" (II, p. 84). It is interesting to watch this maladive sensibility secreting, so to speak, a philosophy which is justified by constant reference to its physical origins. His own variations fascinate and distress the philosopher from the first to the last page of his Journal. They are the raw material out of which he builds a distinctive psychology.

As early as 1794 we find him regretting that Rousseau had not written the book he projected and mentioned in the *Confessions* on the variations which men undergo and which can make them so unlike themselves. "I don't know", he continues, "if there is a man whose existence is so variable as mine.... Is it possible that our feelings, affections and principles depend on certain physical states of our organs? Is reason always powerless against the influence of temperament?" This question leads to the next preoccupation with which his philosophy is concerned—the freedom of the will. He would like to see the will analysed as Condillac analysed the understanding. It would require a philosopher who could frequently turn in upon himself or one who rarely goes out of himself. Unfortunately this aptitude belongs, perhaps, to a state of sickness (I, pp. 35, 36, 37). Another fragment (I, pp. 46, 47) is a record of self-reproaches for not having written the book of his own variations when he had the chance. Had he done so there would now result "le tableau le plus original, le plus varié, et pour moi le plus instructif". He proceeds to describe the conditions in which he has lived—perfect conditions for introspection when practised by one who has so clear a

notion of the ideal requirements of the inner life—
"separation from the body or complete absence of
organic impressions or a perfect balance between them
or their subordination to the authority of the soul" (I,
p. 240). Once again he seems to approach a conception
of the Unconscious. The variations which disturb and
attract him proceed, he suspects, from a region beyond
the power of the will and of the conscious mind. "It
follows from these inner experiences which could be
repeated at any moment, that the phenomena of the
sensibility or, if you prefer, the modifications of the
passive (part of the) soul, succeed one another and,
varying in a thousand ways, constitute the life of sensation without the *ego* having intervened. There is then,
beyond the *ego* and the conscious, and independently
of the life of relation, a series of sensitive phenomena
which become the objects of inner apperception but
which could subsist without it" (I, p. 92).[1]

III

How does Maine de Biran employ his introspective gift?
First in the uncompromising examination of the self, the
annotation and denunciation of defects moral and intellectual. The sense of failure is frequently analysed;
the lack of persistence and concentration is exposed,
and self-confession ends in self-lamentation. As with
Amiel all this tends to recur and to be accompanied by
little improvement. Yet there are gains: "What consoles
me often and makes me believe that I am a little less
sick than others, is that I am deeply aware of all the

[1] Cf. "*Qui sait tout ce que peut la réflexion concentrée, et s'il n'y a pas un
nouveau monde intérieur, qui pourra être découvert un jour par quelque Colomb
métaphysicien?*" (I, p. 253).

52 THE INNER LIFE OF A PHILOSOPHER:

infirmities of my mind and that I often take stock of its maladies" (II, p. 198). Some of these confessions are particularly moving and finely expressed. It is difficult to imagine a more delicate and radical avowal of intimate failure than the original of the following passage: "I have not run like other men after the external goods of fortune; all my expectations have centred in my inner disposition which is under the sway of fortune no less than external goods are. Under an appearance of wisdom and moderation I have been just as blind, inconstant and frivolous as those who are ceaselessly drawn away from themselves by the imagination and the passions" (II, p. 262). And again this: "Nothing but wretched trivialities occupy me; yet formerly I knew *the life of the spirit*, and I still preserve a tendency towards that life; I only half yield, and not without remorse, to whatever turns me from it. Would it not be better always to have been a stranger to it, like so many other men?" (II, p. 285).

Maine de Biran is one of those personal thinkers who, discouraged and incapacitated by their sense of perfection, are yet conscious that their scattered contributions count beyond the achievement of many robust system-makers. Introspection in his case is justified by results. But these results carry the introspective act beyond itself. Ulterior to self-examination is the development of a new science. Progress through the Journal shows the psychologist thinking about his subject quite as often as the meditative man thinking about himself. At one time the emphasis is on the self: "Je cherche toujours ce qui dépend de l'homme, ou plutôt du *moi*, dans telle situation déterminée de l'organisation et de la sensibilité" (II,

p. 182). At another we see the ultimate domination of the philosophic objective. Ruminating vaguely at his fireside on a work of philosophy which he wishes to see in print before he "dies to the world", he decides that the inner life needs cultivating after the immense "extraversion" (as we might say) of the Revolution and the Empire, and he concludes that it is only the desire to know the *true* that involves a man in the descent into the deeper regions of his soul (I, p. 296).

Along with this growth in the *application* of the introspective act there appear from the year 1817 onward signs of a far more profound orientation, affecting the inner life in its moral and spiritual aspects, as well as the philosophical outlook. The transition is finely characterised in the following paragraph, which concludes an entry for 1817: "I die at each moment not only to the world and external pleasures but still more to myself, to my faculties, to this internal life of the *ego* where I formerly found a refuge for meditation, and of which I am disillusioned as with a shadow. There is no more enjoyment in amour-propre. The culture of the mind seems to me a useless burden from which I have nothing more to hope. One must seek one's fulcrum in another world."

"*Il faut chercher son point d'appui dans un autre monde.*" This phrase marks a new departure in the philosopher's inner experience and points to the religious aspiration which pervades the record of the last seven or eight years of his life and floods some of the most impressive passages of the end. An entry which stands for the 26th May to the 6th June 1818 is typical: "... I am composing a philosophic work on moral ideas with ideas of my own which I link laboriously together and which strike me now as elevated and noble, now as trivial; but I do not yet know if I shall succeed in *closing my circle* and terminating a composition worthy to appear before the public: I have no confidence in that.

"Finding nothing in me or outside me, in the world of my ideas or in that of objects which satisfies me, nothing on which I can find support and which gives me any satisfaction, I have been inclined for some time to seek in the notions of absolute, infinite, immutable being that stable *point d'appui* which has become the need of my mind and soul. The religious and moral beliefs, which reason does not *make* but which are a necessary basis and starting-point for reason, offer themselves as my only refuge, and I find no true science save precisely there where formerly, with the philosophers, I saw nothing but reveries and fantasies.

"What I took for reality, for the proper object of science, has now in my eyes only a purely phenomenal value; my point of view has changed with my disposition and moral character. I like to tell myself that this is the perfecting of a part of my being which compensates for the loss of other faculties; but I hope it is so, I believe it to be so, I have no consciousness that it is so. All that by which I felt the immediate pleasure of being alive, of exercising my faculties and living powers has disappeared; I no longer know anything but the serious side of life, from which I seek vainly to distract myself" (II, pp. 100, 101).

"Here reigns mysticism", sighed Victor Cousin disapprovingly when he looked through the private papers of Maine de Biran. The transformation is sealed by the mood of self-reproof which supervenes and marks the abandonment of idle introspection: "I have made myself also a *speculative conscience* by disapproving of certain sentiments or acts to which I used to yield.... The habit of occupying oneself specially with what passes within one, the good and the evil, could this be immoral? I fear so after my experience. One must give oneself an aim, a *point d'appui outside the self* and *higher than the self* in order to react successfully against one's own modifications, while observing and taking stock of them. One must not think that all is said when one's amour-propre is satisfied with a fine observation on a deep discovery made within" (II, p. 245).

Again the problem of the physical and organic conditioning of the mind and personality surges up with renewed violence: "I am conscious that in certain modifications of the animal or sensitive life which I know too well, the predominance or even the exercise of the superior life of the soul becomes impossible" (II, p. 311). One aspect of the problem, generalised though always referred to the self, is to discover the delimitations of the three modes of being, physical, intellectual and spiritual, which occupy much of the philosopher's attention during the last phase. He cannot evade the conviction that the physical, or what he calls the *passive*, substratum conditions the other two. This leads to a further effort to discover the autonomy of the spiritual. And all these considerations and distinctions are themselves conditioned in the thinker by the physical constitution and circumstances which daily affect his mental and spiritual life. It is an intimately tragic, discreet but fascinating drama that we watch reflected in some of the remarkably beautiful passages with which his Journal closes. The acute penetration of the thought diving inward or soaring in perpendicular flight, yet soon brought back to the miseries of earth and the body, leaving nothing but the gesture of aspiration, the exquisite sincerity of the analysis of failure and the transparent distinction and pathos of its record. One feels here the last refinements of self-inquisition, as one does sometimes in Amiel, rarely if ever in Montaigne, never in Rousseau.

"One cannot know beforehand to what degree of moral nullity and disgust with oneself malady can reduce us. I am the living proof of that....I do not think that independently of such dispositions, not of the whole body but of that organic and indeterminate part of which we speak, the soul can be strong in itself. I have the intimate feeling of this miserable dependence; it needs a supernatural influence to alter that" (II, p. 340).

Nowhere in the Journal do we clearly perceive that "repose in the tranquil possession of the Christian faith" which the editor implies was the final attainment of the philosopher's life and quest.[1] "Death terminated his ascent", said Édouard Le Roy, "when he was almost on the threshold of the ineffable experience."[2] To suggest more is to destroy the note of anxious disquietude—never despair but never absolute assurance—which pervades the final pages.

[1] Vol. II, Introduction, p. xxxix.
[2] *Ibid.* p. xxxiii, footnote.

CHAPTER V

SÉNANCOUR'S *OBERMANN*

I

HAVING written two poems directly inspired by the work of Étienne Pivert de Sénancour, Matthew Arnold expressed his esteem for *Obermann* in unmistakable terms when, in a note to the first, he wrote: "To me, indeed, it will always seem that the impressiveness of this production can hardly be rated too high." Later, in an essay on Amiel—petulant but interesting and containing some of the few acute things that have been said in English about the *Journal Intime*—Arnold made his preference for *Obermann* clear, setting it off with one or two examples, happily chosen to support his arguments, though scarcely valid beyond the points they illustrate.

Sénancour's work is largely autobiographical. But for all the investigations that have recently been made, culminating in the contributions of M. André Monglond, it does not seem possible to dissociate with certitude what represents the author's actual existence from what may be called the life of his hero. Not that *Obermann* is in the contemporary sense a *vie romancée*. The phrase has been applied to it, sometimes tentatively, sometimes emphatically; but it is obviously not the story of a life. Events are omitted—the Revolution is not mentioned— or mysteriously alluded to, in favour of moods, impressions and speculations which ultimately divert the author from self-study to essay-writing. M. Monglond claims that the chronology of the work is more exact than it has been thought to be; but he admits that it is posterior by several years to what it recounts. Begun in Paris in 1801 and finished at Agis, near Fribourg, in 1803, *Obermann* was published in 1804. It had no success at the time, being overshadowed by Chateaubriand's *René*, which was reissued in the same year.

The *mélange* of elements which went into its composition was transposed into the epistolary form frequently adopted in the period now called "pre-Romantic". Some resemblance in spirit suggests a debt to Rousseau's last work, *Les Rêveries d'un promeneur solitaire*. This Sénancour had already imitated. His *Rêveries sur la nature primitive de l'homme* was first published in 1799 and fell dead from the press. It was republished with supplements later, just as, it is important for the sequel to notice, the letters of the tenth year were added as a supplement to the second edition of *Obermann* (1833). The same form was used for an early novel called *Aldomen*, which M. Monglond recently brought to light. "Par la forme romanesque", he says, "*Aldomen* est une première ébauche d'*Obermann*, maigre et maladroite, mais singulièrement précieuse. L'un et l'autre sont des romans par lettres. Aldomen communique à un ami le journal de ses méditations, de ses ennuis, de ses chimères. D'histoire, à proprement parler, il n'y en a pas...."[1]

Obermann is here referred to as a novel, and so it has

[1] This and the next two quotations come from A. Monglond, *Vies Préromantiques*: "La Jeunesse de Sénancour", Paris, 1925.

always been classified by historians. But in his prefatory Observations the author denied that the letters were composed with such an intention. "There is in them", he says, "no dramatic movement, no deliberate working up of events, no climax, nothing of what is called the interest of a work." It is difficult to relate *Obermann* to a genre. M. Monglond moreover points out that it is one of a series of works which Sénancour was perpetually recasting: "From one to another he takes up and transposes, with some rehandling, fragments, pages, themes, simple phrases and rhythms, as if each new edition was intended to disavow, to annihilate the editions which preceded it." Obviously the letters of *Obermann* stand at some distance from experience.

With this hybrid production which he admired Arnold contrasts by implication and example a private diary. H. F. Amiel was probably a more complex person even than the author of *Obermann*. For thirty or forty years he had stocked his note-books with elaborate reflections of himself and his ideas. But the complexity of the *Journal Intime* is not increased by its mode of presentation. Compared with the immediacy of the "fragments" directly dictated by the mood and the moment and never revised, the letters of *Obermann* seem products of mannered and confused artifice. Even their occasional simplicity looks suspect. There is this difference too. Amiel's Journal is an unequal compilation from which it is not difficult to make rich selections. The good things in *Obermann* are weighted with so much artistically inferior material that one cannot help admiring the ingenuity of Arnold's selective powers.

The first point which Arnold makes, after comparing a passage on nature from his preferred author with a similar passage from the *Journal Intime*, is that "magic of style is with Sénancour's feeling for nature, not Amiel's". Sénancour has often been praised for his descriptions. But whether readers have instantly and genuinely felt the stylistic superiority of the passage from *Obermann*, or whether most of them have not been overawed by a verdict which seems so sure of itself, is a question that might be worth trying to answer. It is more useful, however, to raise the general question, has *Obermann* style? Of *Obermann* Lanson asserted: "Il n'y manque que le style." In the Observations prefixed to the letters the author himself admitted that their style was unequal and irregular; but he did not pretend to justify it. What are we to say? Our reply shall be guarded. We are more conscious of a style in Sénancour's work than in Amiel's. But we suspect that much of its magic has by now gone the way of the glamour and rhetoric of its period.

Arnold's second point is still more debatable. He was impatient with Édouard Scherer for having said that Amiel's speculative philosophy is "on a far other scale of vastness" than Sénancour's. Here the English critic seems a little inconsistent. Arnold strongly disapproved of what he called Amiel's "philosophy of the Maia and the Great Wheel", because it was unproductive. The selection he used may not have made it clear that this philosophy represents but one strain in Amiel's varied speculations. Anyhow, it seems odd that Arnold should so strenuously have preferred Obermann, whose one conviction, confirmed by his experience and persistently confessed, is that life and effort are futile—

"tout existe en vain devant lui, il vit seul, il est absent dans le monde vivant" (I, p. 92).[1]

II

Writing to the friend who is assumed to be the recipient of most if not all of these letters, Obermann tells him in the sixtieth not to expect historical narratives or the descriptions of an observant and instructive traveller. Being a solitary, he will not speak of men whom his friend frequents far more than he does himself. Having no adventures he will not write the romance of his life. Not what he is surrounded by but what he experiences and feels shall be his theme. This is the real Obermann. "Quand nous nous entretenons l'un avec l'autre, c'est de nous-mêmes: rien n'est plus près de nous." With so clear an idea of what Obermann should do, why does Sénancour allow him to default?

The *motif* of the letters seems to be that mysterious personal ennui which the author, more ingeniously than any of his contemporaries, succeeds in not christening. Instead of having attempted some diagnosis of the malady with which it infected most of the Romantics before and after himself, Sénancour yields, as they all do, to sentimental meditation and sometimes to insipid garrulity on the melancholy theme. His ruminations are not introspection but reverie. At best he gives us adumbrations of his ennui; rarely, if ever, does he attempt analysis.[2]

[1] References are to the edition of *Obermann* published by the *Société des Textes Français Modernes*, vol. I, 1912 (Cornély), vol. II, 1913 (Hachette).
[2] An exception should be made in favour of the *Rêveries sur la nature primitive de l'homme*, especially the Fourth Reverie. What really distracts Sénancour from introspection is revealed by the preoccupation of his

Nothing could be more futile than to intimate to an author, dead for nearly a century, how he should have conceived and carried through a task which has brought him some fame. But we are not attempting to correct Sénancour. We are trying to show why in our opinion so much of *Obermann* is tedious reading to-day. With his brooding habit of thought, uncommon enough with a Frenchman, and the adoption of an intimate prose form, rather than any of those lyrical or dramatic moulds into which his great successors were to pour their feelings, Sénancour might have left something distinct from, and perhaps superior to, the typical French romantic production. His work shows personal distinction. But what qualities and values it possesses are for the most part diluted in lengthy and often exasperating discourses. One reader at least feels impatient at the perpetual evasion of a problem, perpetually alluded to in terms like these: "Il y a dans moi un dérangement, une sorte de délire, qui n'est pas celui des passions: qui n'est pas non plus de la folie: c'est le désordre des ennuis; c'est la discordance qu'ils ont commencée entre moi et les choses; c'est l'inquiétude que des besoins longtemps comprimés ont mise à la place des désirs" (I, p. 91).

Obermann seems full of subterfuges and devices unconsciously adopted to avoid telling us more about this "désordre des ennuis".[1] One of these is to hide behind earliest impersonation: "C'est de moi," declares Aldomen, "de moi seul que je veux m'occuper maintenant: cherchons d'abord comment je puis être heureux et sage dans un état obscur, mais choisi." Cited by A. Monglond, *op. cit.* p. 155.

[1] A paragraph here or there escapes this verdict. But we have found only one section where self-investigation is maintained against the temptation to indulge in reverie and generalisation—the entry dated "3 août", Lettre XLVI (I, p. 209).

a vague poetic formula: "A la vérité, jusqu'à présent du moins, rien de ce qui existe n'a pleinement mon affection, et un vide inexprimable est la constante habitude de mon âme altérée" (I, p. 24). The void, as Sénancour knows, leads nowhere beyond a cliché: "Le vide devient fastidieux à la longue; il dégénère en une morne habitude..." (I, p. 213). His chief faults, however, are to generalise sententiously, to moralise incontinently and to lose his best threads in sombre meshes of rambling speculation in which, it has been said, "il y a du tout". The melancholy itself is too much exteriorised. When not indulged in for its own sake, this "volupté de la mélancolie" degenerates into a vague romantic misanthropy. One is made oppressively to feel that, if anything is not new under the sun, it is the sense of the vanity of things. "A force d'être ennuyé," said Sainte-Beuve, "Obermann court risque à la longue de devenir ennuyeux." All the world can generalise and moralise in this manner. Few men in a century say anything of the kind that endures. The introspective type of writer is not as a rule one of them: his basis is too narrow. This is Sénancour's weakness as a moralist: "Je cherche des données qui m'indiquent les besoins de l'homme; et je les cherche dans moi, pour me tromper moins. Je trouve dans mes sensations un exemple limité, mais sûr; et en observant le seul homme que je puisse bien sentir, je m'attache à découvrir quel pourrait être l'homme en général" (I, pp. 209, 210). Montaigne also tried to discover the secrets of man's nature from a study of the self, but he did not confine his investigations to the basis of his sensations.

Obermann would not be true to the sentimental

tradition had he not pondered on suicide. The forty-first letter is devoted at length to this subject. Its early pages show something of what Sénancour might have done in the analysis of ennui. But soon rhetoric gets the better of him and he is writing like Chateaubriand: "Je songe volontiers à ceux qui, le matin de leurs jours, ont trouvé leur éternelle nuit; ce sentiment me repose et me console, c'est l'instinct du soir" (1, p. 163). The interminable monologue ends with a paragraph in which we detect a touch of unconscious comedy. This pale precursor of Manfred is determined to postpone the deed until it can be done in the grand manner: "...je me hâte moins, parce que dans quelques mois je le pourrai comme aujourd'hui, et que les Alpes sont le seul lieu qui convienne à la manière dont je voudrais m'éteindre" (1, p. 174).

Like the letters of a celebrity in that world which he despises, Obermann's were not written merely to be read in private. Their "vaine éloquence des mots" can irritate even their author (1, p. 170). Yet there are points in their favour which explain their persistent, if diminished, reputation. We shall leave their descriptions of nature on the pedestal where the critics have placed them. What seems not to have been indicated with sufficient emphasis is that several of the shorter letters are charming and almost perfect in tone. Everyone might not agree to apply these epithets to the following, but is it not, so to speak, *Obermann* in epitome?

"Fontainebleau, 14 août, 11.
Je vais dans les bois avant que le soleil éclaire; je le vois se lever pour un beau jour; je marche dans la fougère encore humide, dans les ronces, parmi les biches,

sous les bouleaux du mont Chauvet: un sentiment de ce bonheur qui était possible m'agite avec force, me pousse et m'oppresse. Je monte, je descends, je vais comme un homme qui veut jouir; puis un soupir, quelque humeur, et tout un jour misérable" (I, p. 73).[1]

III

The series was extended to cover a period of ten years. It is noticeable that the latter half is, in contrast to the former, predominantly objective. The longer letters now deal with such themes as the philosophy of numbers, fashions and morals, love, beverages, money and the simple life, physical types, hygiene and maladies óf the Swiss, literary fame. In the forty-ninth the writer carefully distinguishes his position from that of the representatives of Christianity; in the seventieth he discusses the influence of climate on psychology. Some of these letters have points of general interest; others show the author's curious tastes. But they are all, he admits, too much like treatises, and in the supplement which ends the series he writes their condemnation and adds his excuse: "Je dis en beaucoup de paroles ce que j'aurais pu vous apprendre en trois lignes; mais c'était ma manière, et d'ailleurs j'ai du loisir..." (II, p. 233). Even the shorter letters do not now reach the standard of some of the earlier trifles. An exception must be made of the seventy-first, which shows in a slight yet condensed form a skill in the analytic portrait which reminds one of La Bruyère.

Rarely any of these letters from the sixth year

[1] The ninth letter may also be recommended. It is not Obermann at his grandest but it may be Sénancour at his best.

onward dwell on the theme of ennui. When Sénancour returns to it, as in LXXV, he is soon identifying his personal malaise with the "sentiment de la chute et du néant des joies humaines", and once more he borrows a strain from Ecclesiastes. Metaphysical, moralistic, cabbalistic, speculative, the reveries turn most often on happiness and destiny. But now he is far more concerned with the general problem of destiny than with his personal fate, without having anything new or interesting to propound on the larger issue. It is characteristic of this phase that nature means less to him. He has returned to Switzerland, but his taste for complete isolation is lost: "Je ne désirerais pas maintenant une vie tout-à-fait obscure et oubliée dans les montagnes. Je ne veux plus des choses si simples..." (II, p. 39). The disillusionment which lovers of nature have so often felt on looking back to thrills of the past has become the experience of one of the most famous of them. But on this mystery as on so many others of which he seems aware, Sénancour throws no light.

But these letters are not Obermann's. It would be unfair to judge the author on material appended over thirty years after the original letters were written. If Sénancour's positive self-analysis never goes deep, depth of a kind cannot be denied him. He possessed to an incomparable degree that special romantic art, the descriptive analysis of one's own sensibility. "Indicible sensibilité, charme et tourment de nos vaines années; vaste conscience d'une nature partout accablante et partout impénétrable, passion universelle, sagesse avancée, voluptueux abandon; tout ce qu'un cœur mortel peut contenir de besoins et d'ennuis profonds, j'ai

tout senti, tout éprouvé dans cette nuit mémorable..."
(I, pp. 22, 23). That may be too rhetorical; but need one withhold approval from this milder passage because it forms part of the fragment on the word "Romantic" and the *Ranz des Vaches*? "Mais vous, que le vulgaire croit semblables à lui, parce que vous vivez avec simplicité, parce que vous avez du génie sans avoir les prétentions de l'esprit, ou simplement parce qu'il vous voit vivre, et que, comme lui, vous mangez et vous dormez; hommes primitifs, jetés çà et là dans le siècle vain, pour conserver la trace des choses naturelles, vous vous reconnaissez, vous vous entendez dans une langue que la foule ne sait point, quand le soleil d'octobre paraît dans les brouillards sur les bois jaunis; quand un filet d'eau coule et tombe dans un pré fermé d'arbres, au coucher de la lune; quand sous le ciel d'été, dans un jour sans nuages, une voix de femme chante à quatre heures, un peu au loin, au milieu des murs et des toits d'une grande ville" (I, pp. 144, 145).

In such pieces Sénancour is almost entirely original and independent of the contemporaries by whose work his was obscured. Actually he was preceded in the description of altitudes by a Frenchman, Ramond des Carbonnières, who had translated the Letters of William Coxe on Switzerland. One might speculate on the influence these letters may have had on a work whose "discovery" was partly the result of an English critic's enthusiasm. But such ingratiating and perhaps gratuitous side-issues are not our concern. We have attempted to look at *Obermann* from a special angle and to ask what its self-analysis is worth. For us the work suggests a rich potential not fully applied. Sénancour's introspection remained an integral part of his sensations, of his *volupté*, as a man of feeling; it was not used to penetrate below feeling, sensation, *volupté*, to the man. Like the introspection of all romantics it was a form of narcissism.

CHAPTER VI

SOME ROMANTIC POETS

I

THE French Romanticists were orators with a taste for the epic underlying their eloquent effusions. What intimacy there is in their work will be found in the elegiac or passionate strains of their lyricism, not in the efforts they made at more direct forms of expansiveness. In his *Confidences* Lamartine records the most picturesque episodes of his life in fluent paragraphs of romantic prose. The famous episode, *Graziella*, is still published in expensive editions with illustrations which are as unfaithful to the facts as was, apparently, the poet's presentation of them. Alfred de Musset's conception of intimacy was an indiscreet effusiveness. The impulse to tell a story—the self-consciously corrupt and flamboyant sequence of his first *affaires de cœur*—dominates the *Confessions d'un enfant du Siècle*. After twenty pages of feverish speculation he comes to the point with "J'ai à raconter à quelle occasion je fus pris d'abord de la maladie du siècle." The episodes of his amorous initiation are staged as in a melodramatic novel. Violent effects of feeling are described externally, cast in attitudes and clichés without a trace of analysis. An observation made by one of Wyndham Lewis's characters is applicable here: "A man only goes and importunes the world with a confession when his self will not listen to him or recognise his shortcomings."[1] The abundant verve, of course, is there; so is the sign of the poet's undeniable sincerity—his feverish sentimentality divorced from the fancy of the *contes* and comedies and from the *souffle* of the best lyrics.

Gravity and depth are the monopoly of the only Romanticist who had reserve. "Vous trouverez quelque chose là", said Alfred de Vigny a few days before his death, drawing a friend's attention to some note-books in his library. Louis Ratisbonne ultimately published a selection of these fragments under the title of *Journal d'un poète*. A few of the items, such as the visit to Sir Walter Scott or the impressions of Academicians whom Vigny had to canvass, are almost well known. Certain phrases scattered among the rest are accepted as the quintessence of a modern stoic's philosophy of life. Émile Faguet gave some of them a pivotal prominence in that study of the poet which has been a vade-mecum of examinees—and of examiners—for nearly half a century. But these mottoes of concentrated pessimism are isolated in the Journal. They are the "chords of bronze" in a miscellany of private undertones and public references, and their reverberations are lost among pronouncements on politics and literature, sketches and synopses of projected poems, plays and tales.

Vigny's friend was right not to designate as a *journal intime* these notes, which he described as "ces Mémoires de son imagination et de ses pensées". What intimacy they show is not in the thought but in the imagination. It was an acute intuition that prompted a contemporary

[1] Tarr, p. 13.

SOME ROMANTIC POETS 71

to make what sounds like a paradox at the poet's expense. Of Alfred de Vigny Jules Sandeau wrote: "Personne n'a vécu dans sa familiarité, pas même lui." We turn the pages of the Journal for direct personal light on the writer, but find hardly a trace of introspection. Two of the headings give a promise of self-analysis, *Sur soi-même* (1840) and *De moi-même* (1844); but the latter only is worth a glance from our standpoint. I have attempted a translation:

"*What is done* and *what is said* by me or by others has always been of small importance to me. At the moment when the act is done or the word spoken I am elsewhere, I think of something else; *what is dreamt of* is everything to me.

"The better world I wait and pray for continuously, is there.

"It takes long to realise one's character and to explain the *why and wherefore of oneself*.

"I have long suffered the tyranny of this distraction. (But) imagination carries me into a region of delicious and impossible suppositions. What I actually say it makes colder and less felt, because I am dreaming of what I would say or of what I should like to hear myself saying in order to be happier."[1]

This shows clearly the rejection of introspection by a romantic poet. But for more light on the type of imaginative intimacy which Vigny preferred we must turn from his Journal and from the confessions of his peers of the 1830's. One of their contemporaries, an obscure young nobleman whose fame was entirely post-

[1] Delagrave's edition, p. 175. Cf. Nouv. éd. revue et augmentée par F. Baldensperger, London, 1928, p. 195.

humous (mostly the work of Sainte-Beuve and Matthew Arnold), left a brief memento of some of his deeper moods and moments, in exchange for which I should be tempted to give all their ruminations and disclosures.

II

Once, in company, Maurice de Guérin received a letter from a friend out of which fell some wild flowers. This confused him, but thanks to the indifference of those around, the incident passed without comment. To open the *Cahier Vert* in the company of even a sensitive diarist like Amiel is to risk spilling its contents on an unsympathetic parquet. "As for the Journal," he wrote in a fragment on Maurice de Guérin, "it contains delicious passages, but apart from these, it gives no exact idea of the culture, studies, ideas and scope of the man who wrote it. Speaking only in very general terms of the movements of the inner life, it does not delineate a distinct individuality, and above all it does not mark its true proportions or real nature." Amiel insists that a diary treated in this way is an almost impersonal confessional: it does not distinguish one sinner from another. In its lack of biographical and historical detail he sees something deceptive, because the man who wrote it is not represented as specifically different from men of his kind.

The *Cahier Vert* gives few precise details of the "occupations" of its author. But Amiel's approach is too concrete. He fails to notice the particular qualities, the unique charm and distinction of this diminutive diary. The self it reveals is immature, infinitely more restricted than his own; but it is more delicately poised, more wonderfully attractive. This is the journal of a pure sensibility, not, like Amiel's, of a thinking and feeling being; it was kept intermittently for just over three years, not persevered in for thirty or forty. The sensibility is indeed exceptional. There can be no excuse for confusing it, by the implication of a lack of specific quality, with other romantic natures. The absence of regularity, the indifference to facts and events help to make the record appear almost wistfully spontaneous and fresh. But this is an appearance only. Perfection of tone was reached with economy of means but not without effort: one editor complained of the diarist's morbid concern with style. In this sketch-book of the ecstasies and depressions of a poet, almost every one of the entries is the perfect miniature of an inner drama: "J'ai mené mon petit drame sous vos yeux" (p. 165).[1]

Some of his critic's strictures Maurice de Guérin would not have denied. "J'avance bien lentement du côté de l'intelligence", he admits (p. 26). Listening to the music of the sea at night: "Je ne dirai jamais rien qui vaille là-dessus", he confesses, "car je n'entends rien à l'analyse; revenons donc au sentiment" (pp. 92, 93). Yet he can suggest, if he cannot analyse, and he excels at suggesting the effects nature can produce on his sensibility. Here he shows a penetration rare for a French poet. Sometimes in spite of many differences he reminds one vaguely of the author of the *Prelude*. For him too the experience of inwardness was at first associated with nature regarded pantheistically: "O pureté des champs! J'allais sans cesse montant de la nature à Dieu, et redescendant de Dieu à la nature. C'était là ma vie

[1] Édition Crès, 1921.

intérieure mêlée de quelques mélancolies, de quelques tressaillements du cœur..." (p. 115).

Such an attitude could not escape sentimentality. Nature is one of his two "consolatrices". The other is this *cahier*, which he regards as the ideal confidant who understands and comforts, shares and sympathises, his spiritual equal (p. 188). From this mood Guérin saves himself by being a poet, a man of imagination. Sentiment along with the harder facts of experience soon evaporates for him into beauty. Just, he says, as the air likes to condense the emanations of the waters and to fill ⟨with fine clouds, "mon imagination s'empare des évaporations de mon âme, les amasse, les forme à son gré, et les laisse dériver au courant du souffle secret qui passe à travers toute intelligence" (p. 163).

Following the sequence of entries we note at this point the temporary intervention of a new idea indicated in the fragments for July and August 1834. Maurice de Guérin begins to notice within himself something which softens his intimate distress and which he hopes will ultimately raise him in his own eyes—"le progrès de mon âme dans l'amour et l'intelligence de la liberté..." (p. 135). The new fervour of liberty is still strong in the first days of August. But soon the appeal of the city where his enthusiasms are to be worked out slackens. Earlier moods recur. To quit solitude for the crowd, to exchange the vague mystery of nature for "l'âpre réalité sociale", now seems like a return to evil and misfortune.

Where then are we to find a ground of unity in the rare but chaotic sensibility focussed in this miniature of moods? Not, after all, in any relation to externals.

What is real, what is best in Maurice de Guérin is to be sought in the reverse direction—"ma vie intérieure, ce qu'il y a de meilleur en moi" (p. 150). "Nombre de causes", he writes in one of the last entries, "dans ma nature (intérieure) et extérieure, m'ont de bonne heure incliné sur moi-même. Mon âme fut mon premier horizon. Voilà bien longtemps que j'y contemple..." (p. 185).

His desolate reaction from the failure to externalise in response to the war-cry of the time produces some passages which are as fine as anything of their kind to be found in a similar document. Most impressive, perhaps, is the quality of the writing. But this should not obscure the subtlety of a type of analysis which was not what the intellectual Amiel looked for, but which can be felt intuitively at work in the fragment dated the 26th (August). To quote less than the whole would be to destroy the beauty on which for us its significance depends. But we cannot resist the temptation to translate a paragraph from what is perhaps the most important passage in the *Cahier Vert*—that dated the 10th December (p. 158). It is as well written as the other; and it contains, besides, the key idea to the interpretation we offer of the quality of inwardness reflected in this Journal—the identification of the inner life with the imagination:

"I extend and broaden the sense of the word imagination: it is for me the name of the inner life, the collective appellation for the finest faculties of the soul —those which clothe the ideas with the adornment of images, those, likewise, which turning towards the infinite, meditate perpetually on the invisible and picture it with images of unknown origin and ineffable form. That is hardly philosophical and is far removed from the accepted psychologies; but in this respect I trouble little about men and the arrangement they have made of our faculties; I break their systems when they fetter me and I go free, as far from them as possible, to reconstruct a soul and a world according to my taste."

In what follows we find the same thought recurring in clearer and more vivid terms. Imagination, as the diarist has come to realise, is the essence of all his mental activities: "Je regarde courir sur ce papier l'ombre de mes imaginations, flocons épars sans cesse balayés par le vent. Telle est la nature de mes pensées et de tous mes biens intellectuels, un peu de vapeur flottante et qui va se dissoudre...."

The inner life, in Maurice de Guérin's case, was always evaporating into shapes of beauty for the eye, not of the mind but of the imagination, to contemplate and pursue. The notes he left preserve a rare, perhaps a unique, example of what might be called *introspection of the imagination*—a type which expresses itself not through the language of psychological or philosophical analysis but in what is essentially the language of poetry, the medium and instrument of the Imagination (romantically conceived) being applied intuitively to its own nature and function. The result is not the synthesis of poetry, or the prosaic precisions which Amiel desired, but a few precious annotations of the specific moods of a poet's genius.

CHAPTER VII

THE FAILURE OF AMIEL

I

REFERRING to the original editors of Amiel's *Journal Intime*, M. Bernard Bouvier, to whose scrupulous loyalty we owe a fuller and a more representative edition (Librairie Stock, 1922), thanks them for a choice which has raised the author to the front rank of moralists of the French tongue. No one to-day, we are told in the opening paragraph of his introduction, disputes the allocation of so eminent a place to the Swiss diarist, who was hailed on his centenary as one of the boldest explorers, one of the great discoverers of the human soul.

Will the next centenary reiterate that verdict? Amiel, a discoverer, an explorer of the soul, may still be allowed. But can the suggestion that he is an equal of the great French moralists continue to go unchallenged?

M. Bouvier has himself opened a breach in the acceptation of Amiel as exclusively a thinker, contrived with zealous devotion by those first discreet editors. They were Mlle Fanny Mercier, the "chère calviniste" to whom he bequeathed the enormous manuscript of his Journal, and Edmond Scherer, the critic, who began by resisting her appeal to take his friend's literary remains seriously. In choosing "fragments" for publication their object was declared to be simply the reproduction of the moral and intellectual physiognomy of their friend. A

78   THE FAILURE OF AMIEL

passage in the introduction to the new edition describes them engaged in sifting Amiel's thought from the events and poetry of his existence, suppressing the spontaneous, the familiar, the raw and the trivial, and even modifying the vigour of his phrases, with a piety which M. Bouvier calls "industrieuse et funeste". The original selection appeared with the intimation that it was "*not a volume of Memoirs*, but the confidences of a solitary thinker, the meditations of a philosopher for whom the things of the soul were the sovereign realities of existence". And it was in these words and with this emphasis that Amiel's Journal was introduced to English readers by Mrs Humphry Ward in 1885.

In one of the early entries (9th September 1850) Amiel wrote: "Mon vrai nom c'est penseur." The paragraph begins with a statement which indicates the meaning he attached to the word: "Ma force est surtout critique" (I, p. 15).[1] A little later he defined the *penseur* by saying that he is to the philosopher what the dilettante is to the artist (I, p. 19). Far from being an original thinker in the constructive, or even in the critical, sense, the real Amiel is a subtle and diligent commentator on other men's thoughts and on his own impressions and moods. He claimed to be no more than a receptacle of other men's ideas. But this is not to deny that he could assimilate and analyse them with superior skill. "Esprit-protée", he called himself (II, p. 158). And so he was, but within limits. His thinking is by no means always broad. Nor is it so diverse and mobile in sympathy that

[1] The Roman numerals indicate the volume, the Arabic, the page in M. Bouvier's edition. Where the date alone is given, it will suffice for reference.

prejudice, scruple or squeamishness cannot deflect the stream or check its flow. "Amiel", said Scherer, "read everything." The variety of his knowledge used to charm the friends who accompanied the critic every Thursday on a walk to the Salève. But those who approach Amiel through his Journal may discover far more variety in his knowledge than in his mind.

Two obvious differences strike one between the position of Amiel at Geneva in the nineteenth century and that of any of the great French moralists, let us say, of the seventeenth. These were either men of the world—a nobleman like La Rochefoucauld or a bourgeois in the service of a nobleman like La Bruyère—immersed in the life of a great social and cultural epoch. Or they were men of religion like Pascal in the first half of that century or Fénelon in the second (neither specifically a "moralist", but each with at least as great a claim as that made on behalf of the diarist), supported by one form or another of the psychological experience of Catholicism.

Amiel's situation, in casual contact with a middle-class circle of relatives and friends and a narrow circle of suspicious colleagues, puts him for social opportunity at the antipodes from a La Rochefoucauld; while his Protestantism with its Puritan morality and Hegelian metaphysics limits his psychological range as compared with the scope of a Fénelon or a Pascal. The conditions of a mind, the circumstances of a life cannot of course be taken in themselves as definite criteria of greatness or inferiority in the person concerned. But it is difficult to conceive of a man as being a great moralist without superior means of seeing and knowing his fellows than were afforded this retiring academic—"classé parmi les

80 THE FAILURE OF AMIEL

professeurs à fuir" (II, p. 139)—constrained to live and work in a city which at times he detested. To make the comparison more personal would be to emphasise the distinction between Amiel and any of those moralists of whom it is implied that he is a peer. Pascal, La Rochefoucauld, Fénelon, La Bruyère knew men in their actions and affairs or, as confessors and consultants, in the intimacy of their religious needs. Amiel's direct knowledge of human nature cannot be compared in breadth or variety with theirs. He knew men chiefly through books. Only himself he knew deeply at first-hand. As a psychologist his sphere is introspection. Yet even here he is great with a difference. Montaigne has shown that the study of the self can become a measurement of common humanity. But as Mayor of Bordeaux, confidant of a king and citizen of Rome, the Essayist had unusual opportunities for knowing at first-hand a diversity of men, nakedly revealed in the light of a turbulent epoch.

Rather than risk the contrast with a French moralist of the *grande espèce*, would it not be wiser to choose for comparison one of Amiel's race and time? Alexandre Vinet, for instance. "Je n'ai jamais senti comme aujourd'hui", wrote the diarist in 1852, "ma parenté d'esprit avec Vinet, le psychologue moraliste, le critique divin et juge" (I, p. 55). And we may apply to Amiel the judgment he passed on his compatriot, that the individualism which was his title to fame was also the cause of his weakness: "On retrouve toujours chez lui le solitaire et l'ascète" (I, p. 56). In the last decade of his life the discouraged diarist admitted the limits of his contacts and outlook: "En restant dans sa chambre, selon le conseil de Pascal, on ne sait jamais ce qu'on peut, et n'ayant aucune mesure de sa valeur sociale, on ne se risque plus parmi les hommes" (II, p. 123). The result of such confinement was a gradual contraction of sympathy, which can hardly be considered a qualification for the role gratuitously allotted to Amiel by some of his admirers. "L'État et l'Église m'ennuient à peu près également", he wrote in 1872. "Je n'ai aucune considération pour le public, aucune admiration pour mon temps. Je goûte la science certaine et j'aime les belles âmes. Voilà ce qui me reste de mes voyages à travers le monde et les choses" (II, p. 32).

II

A test of the moralist lies in the value of his objective judgments on mankind and the ways of the world. Amiel's Journal abounds in examples of the genre. But apart from literary criticism, which Matthew Arnold regarded as his true, but neglected, vocation, most of the ruminations on external themes appear undistinguished and even facile—they can descend to the vaguest of moralising raptures—compared with the penetrating and sometimes profound pieces of introspective analysis. The diarist's true orientation was inward. But in that direction, too, the obstacles we have already adumbrated stood in the path of complete self-investigation. Not only were his religious foundations, his philosophical outlook, the angle from which he saw the world, fatally circumscribed and unfavourably set for the development of a moralist's insight into men and affairs; during the greater part of his life they embarrassed the psychologist in the intimate discovery of the self.

Amiel has described himself as philosophically a Hegelian; and we may describe what religion he thought he had as Hegelian Protestantism. His mind is dominated by an Absolute and an Infinite which seem for him equivalent to the Divine. "Il n'y a repos d'esprit que dans l'absolu, repos du sentiment que dans l'infini, repos de l'âme que dans le divin", runs an entry for the 18th November 1851. "Rien de fini n'est vrai, n'est intéressant, n'est digne de me fixer. Tout ce qui est particulier est exclusif, tout ce qui est exclusif me répugne. Il n'y a de non exclusif que le Tout; c'est dans la communion avec l'Être et par tout l'être que se trouve ma fin...." Thinking and living for Amiel are ultimately regulated by an abstraction. God is a moral absolute whose witness is conscience and whose commands are duty. Amiel reveres this kind of God, at least during the first half of his life. But he never succeeds in feeling that he has done his duty to Him. He frequently calls upon Him. But we rarely or never feel that he is speaking to or of a Person. It is God, the Categorical Imperative, a personification with as little definite or realisable personality as possible beyond a will of its own, it is this metaphysical figment that haunts Amiel's thoughts and hinders his life. For such a religion, if genuinely held and observed without compromise by a pure and elevated nature, may incapacitate for living. It can hold its victim high and dry, suspended above existence during the impressionable, idealistic, formative period, and it can leave him high and dry, without the practice of experience when he comes to middle age. The maturity of such a life will be a ripening of disillusion and regret for lost opportunities.

THE FAILURE OF AMIEL

Thus the intelligent, gifted, amiable, fastidious Amiel is doomed to be a moralist after all—an inconclusive moraliser, *ad infinitum* and, the persistent reader may find, *ad nauseam*; preaching to himself first, then to the world; and preaching always from within the four walls of his study and the pulpit of his private journal.[1] Restlessly his thought fluctuates through the narrow range of his deepest moods, churning an intimate problem which his training and type of mind have imposed on his conscience and which his hypertrophied and harassed conscience can neither effectively deal with nor dismiss. Its solution he misinterprets as a resort to action: "Pourquoi toujours du bavardage et de la phrase, des regrets ou des bâillements, et jamais une action?" (I, p. 124). Throughout life he is haunted by the quest of a vocation. Some of the finest passages in the Journal are analyses of procrastination. On such themes as these he delivers himself the most persistent and the most ineffectual of sermons, recognising the vanity of the preacher, attempting to grasp the cause of his ineffectualness, but as often as not analysing it wrongly, or if not wrongly, superficially, by substituting effects for cause: incredulity, timidity, laziness, discouragement, distrust, irony and the horror of being duped. Then by a rare hazard of acute penetration he strikes home, opening the wound and laying the mischief bare: "Je crois que l'Absolu t'a

---

[1] So many of the entries are hortatory in style! The editor of the recent French edition admits their monotony. It is probable that the larger the choice made from the original of 16,900 pages, the more this defect will strike the reader. But the diarist's justification is here: "J'ai du reste trouvé de la monotonie dans ces pages, et le même sentiment y revient trois ou quatre fois. Tant pis; ces pages ne sont pas faites pour être lues, elles sont écrites pour me calmer et me ressouvenir" (I, p. 36).

rendu pour jamais incapable de t'éprendre des choses relatives, il t'a dégoûté de l'individualité, de ton individualité du moins. Tu n'as vécu dès lors que par complaisance, ne pouvant prendre au grand sérieux une manière de voir ou d'agir ou d'être, qui n'est qu'un point de la série, qu'une forme de l'infini. C'est Hegel à qui tu dois cette indifférence fondamentale, cette objectivité fatale à la vie pratique, cette impossibilité de vouloir fermement ce que tu ne peux croire qu'à demi vrai, bon, utile. Le besoin de totalité t'a fait prendre en pitié le rôle de partie infinitésimale. Le sentiment de l'idéal, du parfait, de l'éternel, en un mot de l'absolu, t'a découragé pour jamais.—Le devoir reste; mais l'illusion enthousiaste a disparu.—Or le dévouement sans un peu de retour, le travail sans un peu d'illusion sont deux choses héroïques, et pour rester constamment héroïque, il faut une foi ardente, une religion ferme, et foi et religion vacillent perpétuellement chez toi.—*O du armer!*" (I, pp. 149, 150).

Are we mistaken in seeing here one of the dangers of the Protestant metaphysic, the danger which threatens the private conscience from predicating the Absolute with such logical intensity that it becomes vitally impracticable, something beyond God and man?—"le grand Tout, plus vaste encore que Dieu, puisque Dieu comme esprit est opposé à un homme et comme éternel est opposé au monde" (II, p. 121). By 1875, when he wrote that phrase Amiel had become indifferent. Eight years before the tone had been poignant: "La soif de l'infini n'est pas étanchée. Dieu est absent" (I, p. 223).

God was to remain absent. The later reflections show a gradual progression towards scepticism and natural-

THE FAILURE OF AMIEL 85

ism. "L'existence de Dieu et l'immortalité de l'âme, ces deux prémisses de la morale religieuse, sont en effet devenues pour toi des thèses incertaines, et le non-souffrir, le moins-souffrir sont demeurés le seul but de l'existence ainsi dépouillée" (II, p. 109). That smacks of epicureanism and this of dilettantism: "Il est certain que je m'éloigne lentement du stoïcisme et que je dérive vers le nonchaloir de Montaigne" (II, p. 296). Had he lived to a "ripe" age the Christian idealist might have become a confirmed Positivist: "Si du moins je croyais à une Providence individuelle!...Le Dieu que les religions mettent dans le ciel et hors de nous n'est peut-être qu'au fond de nous-mêmes" (II, p. 125).

In that long transition through which the modern world seems destined to pass from a supernatural Catholicism to a naturalistic religiosity, Amiel is the rare example of a sincere and sensitive victim skilfully investigating his feelings as he drifts through the Protestant twilight from heaven to earth.

III

Readers with a taste for psychology will have guessed that metaphysics was not the whole of Amiel's problem or perhaps its root. But it may have been worth while to note how his failures are related to that sublimated disorder which one of his first admirers diagnosed and popularised as the "maladie de l'idéal".[1] From such intimate revelations as those which editors have hitherto allowed to reach the public, it will have been perceived that Amiel was much of a sentimentalist. A malicious

[1] The phrase is E. Caro's. M. Bouvier refers to Amiel's "maladie de la pudeur" (Introduction, p. xli).

little essay might be written on the fatuity of Amiel, his immature fastidiousness, his luxurious self-incriminations, his maudlin self-reproaches, his solemn self-upbraidings: "Ne pas te prendre au sérieux, c'est faire un affront à Dieu qui a permis à son saint esprit de résider en toi, et qui attache à ton âme le même prix qu'à la plus privilégiée de toutes..." (I, p. 83). And this is not merely the gravity of youth. At fifty-two he could return from an evening party which his "verve drolatique" had saved from dullness and, before retiring, take himself seriously to book for having been so indecorously amusing! (II, p. 87). And at all times he could be expansive in the dainty, suave manner of the well-bred youth of the last century, indulging in nice reverie about the young woman he met at a party or longing, when the moon is full above the lake, for that young woman or another to be there hanging upon his arm.

A ruthless psychologist of the modern school might have concluded that Amiel had the "complex characteristic of his type", and have deplored the scruples which kept him from more thorough confession. Such speculation and regret would now be vain. Amiel's gradual realisation of another aspect of his spiritual impasse in the stages of his sexual liberation has been revealed in a volume of new selections from the original manuscript, translated by Mr Van Wyck Brooks under the title of *Philine* (Constable, 1931).[1] This selection is concerned almost exclusively with the diarist's amorous life; and it may be regretted that Amiel, who had many sides and whose real distinction it is to have succeeded

[1] *Philine* was first published in France (*Écrits Intimes*, 1927). The English translation contains some additional passages and notes.

in leaving some record of them all, should have been deprived of recognition for the courage and completeness of his self-revelation by being shown to the world in a kind of perpetual partial eclipse or, as it were, facet after facet. First the grave moralist, then the platonic amorist, now the realist in love, capable at times of a candour quite disconcerting.

In a paragraph of M. Bouvier's edition under the date of 14th December 1849, Amiel records the wish to raise an altar to what he apostrophises as "Virginité virile". He adds: "Si c'est une niaiserie, je t'en remercie, mon Dieu." Ten years later he writes: "How strongly I have felt that purity was a sort of heroism, that virginity was a sort of sanctity!" (*Philine*, 14th April 1859).[1] But that this has become an ideal of the past is clear from the entry for 10th July of the same year: "A distinct change, however, which I noticed since the last crisis, is how greatly the mysterious horror of every sexual relation has diminished in me....The coat of mail of Puritan habits, the hair shirt of anxieties and precautions, grows slack and falls away like loosened armour. I become again like a bird, like a savage, like a child at the beginning of puberty. Is this a good thing? Is it a bad thing...?"

On 6th October 1860 he records that he has received a woman's favour and gravely adds: "It was like a bucket of cold water." By the end of the month he can look at the matter philosophically. "The great difference", he writes on the 30th, "that I notice in myself, in this matter, is that the cycle of physical pleasure appears

---

[1] Quotations from this selection are given in Mr Brooks' translation, with the date of entry, the original edition of *Philine* not being easily procurable in this country.

to me as a natural and universal phenomenon and that I judge it with philosophical impartiality instead of seeing it, as formerly, a delirious temptation or a shameful indecency. The naturalistic point of view takes precedence over the moral." Then with a characteristic *revirement* he adds: "But the latter is returning little by little."

The entry for 25th February 1861 is one of Amiel's important pronouncements on the subject. It begins: "Sexuality has been my Nemesis, my torment, since childhood." After enumerating his failings, he continues: "...all this is derived from the primitive shame, from the idealisation of the forbidden fruit, in short, from a false idea of sexuality....That error has poisoned my life. It has hindered me from being a man, and indirectly, it has caused the failure of my career." A little later he writes: "14th July 1861. The moral hurt that was given my childhood by a precocious and sinister idea of sex—can it be that it is remedied only now? I have returned to simplicity after thirty years of distortions, temptations and anxieties. What a singular Odyssey! In the case of others, the first infraction of purity destroys them; with me the first infraction of continence cures me."

Psychologists have now proof of the priority of the sexual in the order of Amiel's troubles and failures. But in his own conscious analysis he maintains that he was deterred from fulfilment in this sphere by the same obstacles that baulked achievement on the other planes. "Je suis mystique en amour; l'infini seul me tente", was the motto of his platonic adolescence. But even then he recognised that the ideal had prevented him from living.

THE FAILURE OF AMIEL

On the 1st of April 1871, in his forty-ninth year, Amiel rounds upon his Christian training as ultimately responsible for the most intimate failure of his life:

"The most serious question of pedagogy and macrobiotics is the sexual function, which also lies at the heart of morals. I believe that it has not been solved either by the educators or by the moralists or by custom.... What is the meaning of these hesitations, of this false shame, when it is a question of the very foundations of our morals? They mean that, on this cardinal point, the doctrine of the Church is troubled and contradictory. The Church is not sure that virginity is not better than marriage and that woman is not synonymous with the temptation of the Evil One, of the Devil; that the first embrace of Adam and Eve, from which humanity was born, is not synonymous with the Fall, and that sexuality is not impurity. It has not repudiated the Oriental and Gnostic idea, and to it the spirit is the very opposite of the flesh and of nature. Therefore, it is embarrassed at the question of love and has contradicted itself many times. It deifies maternity, but prefers virginity, and to reconcile everything, it places on the altar a Virgin-Mother, which naturally depreciates and stigmatises all mothers who are not virgins. In this permanent ambiguity we recognise an unhealthy first view of things, an imperfect conception of nature, an ascetic theology —that is, a violent one, born of reaction and not of contemplation, consequently a half-truth. Since the Church has vacillated as to the doctrine of sex, of nature, of life, and in consequence of love, a sort of anarchy has resulted in men's minds and the discomfort of uncertainty has created hypocrisy and affectation. It is rather the judicial and lay conscience that, following the school of the naturalists and philosophers, has freed itself from the hesitations of the clergy.... The whole of Greek and Latin Christianity is dying out from falsity, and represents the anti-nature phase of the religion of Jesus; it is above all the negation of paganism. It sets earth outside of heaven, and Nature outside of order; it teaches only a relative truth, which is half an error."

That such an outburst should have come from the virtuous Amiel makes it one of the most dramatic, one of the most tragic, confessions in his Journal. Throughout the record he has left us, he often writes like a man oppressed by a burden which is somehow greater than his own. It is as if a civilisation which never admitted failure had become conscious, through him, of the void of its metaphysics, the insecurity of its religious foundations, the precarious virtue of its proudest acquisitions, moral as well as material.

The *Journal Intime* is the posthumous vindication of a man who was unable to prove his superiority even to himself. In its voluminous pages a discouraged writer patiently buried his talent. To us they reveal a master, *the* master perhaps of pure introspection. No one as intelligent as Amiel could practise that art so persistently without profit to himself or without producing something precious. "Mon privilège," he wrote as early as 1852, "c'est d'assister au drame de ma vie, d'avoir conscience de la tragi-comédie de ma propre destinée." And before his death he had glimpsed the assurance that this line of least resistance, this *péché mignon*, this desultory but relentless annotation of the ripples and eddies of a life that ebbed so uneventfully away was his vocation, his justification, his unbelievable *magnum opus*. Morals, philosophy, scholarship, criticism, it is not in any of these things that the singular greatness of the Journal lies. It is the record itself with its slow evolution, its infinite, even when so often reiterated, detail, which is, I suppose, unique in the literature of scrupulous, disconnected autobiography. "The inner life" (I translate from an entry made two years before the end) "opened all its avenues to him. He was able, for recreation, to write fifteen thousand pages of reflections in which reverie communes with itself unrestrained. All that should count."

CHAPTER VIII

THE PARADOX OF LITERARY
INTROSPECTION

I

OUR specimens have been chosen from a host of autobiographers because they appeared to offer the purest and most genuine examples of their kind—authors of a type of journal which aims at being intimate, diarists who would consider it an essential part, if not the central motive, of their habit to withdraw from externality and to attempt introspection. Differences of character, mentality and status, as well as of period and occupation, distinguish each. But one trait, uningratiating enough, seemingly superficial yet insistent, strikes us as common. They are all men of indifferent health, afflicted early or later in life with maladies from which most of them die before they have reached the average span. They include Montaigne, a fact which warns us against generalisations. But it is also a fact that the Essais became intimate from the time when their author began to suffer from the stone and that much of what he wrote subsequently, including the Travel diary, is concerned with his "colique".

"When one does not suffer, one hardly thinks of oneself. Sickness or the reflective habit is required to force us to descend into ourselves. Hardly any but sick people feel themselves to exist.... Health projects us on to external objects, malady brings us back into ourselves" (I, p. 35). So wrote that chronic, self-mastering, active, aspiring, despairing invalid who claimed that malady had made him a psychologist. Maine de Biran and the others—Sénancour, Maurice de Guérin and Amiel— are all in different degrees *malades*. In the moral sphere it is markedly the sense of defects, degeneration, failure, along with moods of self-reproach and self-pity, which forces them to the analysis of motive. In the physical, the torments of a Daudet, for instance, as reflected in that terrible document, *La Doulou*, dictate the most personal jottings of all.

Such experiences compel diagnosis. We must attend to them in order to dispose of them; and if they cannot be disposed of or palliated, they must be borne, and the brunt is in ourselves. "Celui qui souffre", said Amiel, "ne peut imaginer qu'il ne souffre pas; il est ramené à un point particulier, il redevient subjectif" (II, p. 138). Pain usually makes the patient self-conscious in a way that pleasure does only in the case of exceptionally analytical minds. Or it may be that an altogether too remote problem is set by one's feelings of pleasure. The examples we have considered seem at least to have been most intimately themselves when reduced by malady or malaise to self-diagnosis. Such a conclusion—although to record the truth at so depressed a level points to a kind of superiority—does not flatter the minds we have in view. It tends to assimilate some of the most authentic parts of their disclosures to the whimperings of spirits who "come back" in séances.

There is, of course, a point on which the confessor at all times, and the modern psychologist in particular, has insisted—the inherent curative power of the process of analysis. In all the cases we have mentioned, the Journal has become a confidant, sometimes a comforter and a consolation. This is a sentimental role, but its obscure *raisond'être* is remedial. From the medley of explanations in which Amiel indulges towards the end of his life we select this as significant: "The chief utility of the *Journal Intime* is to restore the integrity of the mind and the equilibrium of the conscience, that is, inner health" (II, p. 246). The keeping of an intimate diary can become a kind of catharsis.

One may dislike, one may be wise to reject, the assumption of the role of malady in introspection, when presented in a crude form. But its converse seems unavoidable. Normal conditions do not produce the *journal intime*; nor does success. "When George Sand was normal she did her work. Whenever she lost her poise she wrote a journal. This manifestation of pent-up feelings seeking relief repeated itself several times in her life." Not that what has been published of the *Intimate Journal of George Sand*[1] need detain us. As a record of disillusionment it has the faults which characterise—one might say which "compose"—the *Confessions* of that "child" of genius who had been her lover. It is full of the rhodomontade of romantic expansiveness. The feelings were no doubt genuine. But their tumult has been oiled into a characterless rhythm of clichés by the irresistible "style coulant".

The great, like the successful, writer seems to make an inferior introspective, his intimate thoughts and re-

[1] The quotation comes from p. 19 of a translation published by Williams and Norgate, London, 1927.

actions being dominated by the *faculté maîtresse*. The contents of a poet's diary tend to be what they are (with exceptions) in Coleridge's case, fragments of the *Anima Poetae*. The great critic in his intimacy is a more acute and unguarded, perhaps a more biased and prejudiced, almost certainly a more personal and indiscreet, critic and judge. The virulent notes which Sainte-Beuve reserved under the label of *Mes Poisons* are for the most part objective judgments on the lives and works of others. They fall outside our survey along with most of Baudelaire's fragmentary remains, which have similar characteristics of vindictive objectivisation with but a few exceptions. These are worth a glance.

In the preface to his edition of Baudelaire's intimate writings (Schriffin, 1930), M. Charles Du Bos admits that the two fragments he brought together under that designation—*Fusées* and *Mon Cœur mis à nu*—have the character of scattered notes such as are jotted down in a *carnet*; they show nothing of the sequence of entries made in a diary. He claims, however, that perhaps nothing of the kind exists having such a degree of intimate quality as the end of *Mon cœur mis à nu*. This was to have been an important *opus*, the repository of the poet's verdicts on society and his contemporaries, a testament of vengeance, "un livre de rancune". It would have made Rousseau's *Confessions* pale in comparison; it would doubtless have out-venomed Sainte-Beuve's reservations. But the spleen that inspired it suddenly runs dry: "J'ai cultivé mon hystérie avec jouissance et terreur. Maintenant, j'ai toujours le vertige, et aujourd'hui, 23 janvier 1862, j'ai subi un singulier avertissement, j'ai senti passer sur moi le vent de l'aile de l'imbécillité."

From the relative objectivity of vindictive observations and critical *aperçus*, we are plunged into a despairing intimacy of self-accusations, exhortations and anxieties for common domestic contingencies. The change of tone pivots on a date—the first full date recorded. It marks a premonition of the malady which will destroy the poet within a few years, and which transforms the last pages of his note-book into a poignant *journal intime*.

The worst obsession that haunts Baudelaire for the brief space corresponding to what remains of the diary is not different in kind from one of Amiel's sorest problems. It is the problem of concentration in its most morbid form, as it presents itself to the type which M. Du Bos calls the "aboulique conscient". Baudelaire's despair far surpasses Amiel's in urgency and terror. "Hygiène. Conduite. Morale." The injunctions repeat themselves with a terrible, futile insistence, now that it is too late. Physical and moral anguish can be watched at work, forcing the mind in upon itself. All other preoccupations yield to concrete projects for temporal redemption, for definite achievement, for tasks and payments. The disdainful poet's prose has an unpredictable dying fall. Its timbre wilts as it is applied to those bourgeois themes *par excellence*—concern for a livelihood, anxiety for the material welfare of a mother and a mistress.

II

It was Barrès who launched the fame of Marie Bashkirtseff's Journal. But Barrès himself could not have popularised the more powerful Journal of Marie Lenéru. It resists advertisement, yet it should be better known.

It has nothing of the tremulous charm and vivacity of the Russian girl's diary; it is not half so romantically tragic. Marie Lenéru had a book and a play to her account before she died at forty-three in the year of the Armistice. Marie Bashkirtseff would gladly have given a year of her briefer existence to have produced a prize canvas. But her tragedy seems juvenile and dappled with operatic effects when compared with the grim, undramatic monotone of Marie Lenéru's isolation. One is the tragedy of phthisis, the other the tragedy of deafness.

The Frenchwoman's circumstances were easy, offering no stimulus or necessity to forget or evade her condition. "Nothing worse than what has happened to me can happen," she wrote, "or in a worse way: *souffrance de luxe* which neither kills nor exempts from other ills."[1] Forced by her mother to keep a diary from the age of ten, she had to abandon it in 1890. An abyss of three years, during which she lost her hearing, separates her first attempt from the second: "The life of a happy woman is lost for me. I must invent another in which these frightful years can find a place." She determines to become a writer and prepares for the vocation by strenuous reading. For occasional relief she turns to her Journal and also for self-enlightenment. "Writing", she notes, "is for me a real way of reading myself, in the course of which I often come across much more of the unexpected than in even an original book.... One must write to exist, to become oneself." But her boredom is intolerable. No one, certainly none of the Romantics

[1] *Le Journal de Marie Lenéru*, 2 vols. pp. 351, Crès, 1922. The first volume is the more personal; nearly all our quotations come from it.

whose stock-in-trade was ennui, has made this specific malady—and motive force—of the introspective more terribly convincing than the woman who wrote: "Non seulement je m'ennuie, mais je ne cesse pas de m'ennuyer."—"Je n'écris que dans la sincérité de l'ennui"; and who defined ennui as the state of grace of the sceptic.

But if in its calm, terse way this is a more harrowing record of boredom than any similar document, it reveals perhaps a finer resistance. The Journal of Marie Lenéru is not so much a study of the self as the memorial of a ısuperb moral effort to make something of herself, crippled and incarcerated in silence as she was. It is free from the *péché mignon* that besets the genre: the itch to disburden and confide. Desperate disclosures escape her guard, yet there is no lack of reticence, no trace of sentimentality. The trivialities involved in the habit of keeping a diary find no place in these incisive notes.

Reference is made to Amiel's Journal and there is at least one resemblance—the stress on the Will. But it is Amiel who is, in comparison, the woman. He could never have confronted his anguish thus: "One must not suffer: one must never suffer, but react; and reaction is not patience, still less resignation." To call her acceptance "stoical" would be gratuitous. Her tone is always personal: "Yes, I put all my patience and the ingenuity of a Chinese into the art of hoping...I love life as it is." She refuses to be like Amiel, good only for writing one's journal all one's life!

Hers is the direct outcome of affliction—a clear case of maladive motivation. She calls her note-book "la collection de mes migraines mentales". "Not that I deny them," she adds, "I am nothing without them, but I haven't the patience to look back over my present life, except in my bad moments. Otherwise I work and forge ahead." She insists: "I write in my bad moments when at all costs one must react. Then I assert myself; I feel the need to date, to see some trace of all the invisible toil which is my life and which goes on so buried, so unexpressed that it gives me vertigoes of solitude."

After the complete loss of hearing, which she deplored as the cruellest of disabilities, her sight was threatened. But her eyes were saved and she felt that their improvement reconstituted life for her. "How could I doubt", she asks herself, "the way in which life is made? With my organs I lost my soul. I regain it as I recover them." This pressing yet reluctant sense of the dependence of the self on the physical organism reminds one of the anxious ruminations of Maine de Biran.

One more of Marie Lenéru's thoughts should be noticed because it corrects a bias in our argument. A reconsideration of the roles of pleasure and pain may help to introduce it. The conclusion to which our illustrations appear to point is that all private or spontaneous introspection is introspection of the *suffering* self. But it is obvious that while pain makes us sensitive to ourselves, it also prompts the desire to escape, to forget ourselves. Anguish, malady, affliction concentrate, but they also alienate, the self. They may simply make one aware of oneself as of a tooth that aches. Opposed to the feeling of self-possession, a centrifugal impulse arises, to which one yields as eagerly as to the "freezing" or removal of the molar which has revealed its presence in one's mouth. These commonplaces are at some distance from the thought in question. But a similar conception seems to underlie Marie Lenéru's insistence on the feeling of self-assurance given by what she calls "sensations de luxe". "For myself," she wrote, "I am an absentee; it takes an effort to remember myself. I perceive now that what keeps us in life, makes us inhabit our bodies, gives our balance in space and time, enables us to breathe our consciousness into present things are *sensations de luxe*.... C'est la vision de luxe, la vue large et profonde qui nous installe dans la vie, dans nous-mêmes..." (II, pp. 178, 179).

"Souffrances de luxe", "sensations de luxe". The apparent contradiction at which we have arrived seems to come from a too exclusive insistence on the *physical* conditions of the introspective habit. A broader selection, a closer scrutiny of this motive in relation to others, would no doubt relieve it of much of the implied stigma of malady. Yet habitual introspection could never, I think, be considered a normal or natural use of our faculties. It presupposes, not a misdirection, but a re-direction of energies which would normally have taken an outward course. Observation, investigation, inspection become, in certain circumstances, *intro*spection. But what conditions, if not physical, deflect the flow and turn it back upon itself? When faced with similar question in his own experience, Mr Middleton Murry suggested "thwarted aspiration"; and that I think is the key. If we substitute the idea of *obstruction* for that of *affliction*, we acquire a category which will cover the cases considered here without being limited to their specific pathological reference.

It is difficult to evade the category of an "introspective type", whether we think of such a type as the sporadic emergence of a rare species or as produced and moulded by circumstances operating on more or less favourable predispositions. The Introspective is not a hero or a man of action; he is not a "genius", except perhaps posthumously, and he is never a success. He scarcely qualifies for the popular compliment "manly"; he looks like a malingerer, he is probably maladive, if not a little morbid. If the question of his normality arises, he may be judged supernormal in one or two ways—in a kind of concentration, for instance, which some would prefer to call perseverance or perversity. Otherwise, as a man judged by ordinary standards, he is in danger not so much of appearing abnormal as of being thought *sub*normal—less than the average in application and adaptation, feeble with men, incompetent with women, a bungler at "life".

Such, apparently, is the being who by his very deficiencies, his limitations, his defeatism seems best qualified to tell us what we are like *from within*. And if we want the introspection of the amateur, that is Introspection spontaneous and incarnate, our choice is limited to him; and we are caught in a dilemma. For we do not like his type; we feel its defects; we do not want to hear about the self of such a person. It is his opposite who intrigues us. But he, alas, is too much occupied with being himself to have the time or the technique for analysis or explanation. Heroes, artists, statesmen, promoters, philanderers, bookies, gangsters are all engaged on full-time jobs. How perplexed, how infuriated they would be by a request to step aside and tell us what they are apart from their function! But, it may be interjected, harking back to lending-library stocks, these are the very people who in their "off" moments or in the "evening" of their thoughts turn the retrospect of their exploits and excitements into healthy, saleable literature; they rank next to the novelists as the producers of our age. Yes; but what they produce are, I contend, biographies in the first person. The "doer of our inmost deeds" is not revealed in so business-like a fashion. Is he ever revealed? The important question, I admit, is whether what we look like from within is what we really are—whether in the last resort one is likely to know oneself otherwise than as an engrossing or a debilitated function.

CHAPTER IX

IN SEARCH OF THE SELF

"L'accès à moi-même, oui, là est le nœud de la question."
CH. DU BOS.

THE repugnance one feels for the Scylla of maladive motivation seems but a slight embarrassment compared with the misgivings which arise from gazing into the Charybdis of "pure" introspection. If our examples prove anything it is the rareness and the extraordinary difficulty of thinking about the self. Can the self be the direct object of thought? When the evasive germ has been tracked to its inmost cell, can it be observed there except when it wriggles in the throes of a thought? These are questions as old at least as modern philosophy. Among the many answers that have been given, here is one which is worth recording if only because it preoccupied Maine de Biran. Condorcet is commenting on a *pensée* of Pascal.

"This phrase, to see only ourselves, makes no sense. What sort of man is he who does not act and yet is supposed to contemplate himself? I say not only that such a man is mad and useless to society; but that such a man cannot exist. For what would he be contemplating? His body, his feet, his hands, his five senses? Either he would be an idiot or he would make use of all these things. Would he remain contemplating his faculty of thought? But he can only contemplate that faculty by exercising it. Either he will think of nothing or he will think of the ideas which have already come to him, or he will form new ones; but he can only have ideas from outside. Here he is then necessarily occupied either with his senses or with his ideas; drawn out of himself or imbecile. I repeat, it is impossible for human nature to remain in this state of imaginary torpor; it is absurd to think of it; senseless to lay claim to it. Man is born for action, as fire tends upward and a stone downward...."[1]

Have we then been asking an idle question? To what extent is any one even of our select few definitely committed to the direct investigation of the self, which has been our touchstone? Are we not forced to admit that the immediate concern of the introspective is a far simpler project—to keep a diary of his inner life; and that it is merely the emphasis on inner as differentiated from outer—occurrence, interest, orientation—which distinguishes him? Let us consult the most explicit of introspectives once more and inquire what were the purpose and objective of Amiel's devotion to his *Journal Intime*.

"Pour le moment", he writes in 1852, "ce Journal est encore un être mystique et hybride, semainier, agenda, procès-verbal, inquisiteur, confident, garde-notes, mais où deux rôles dominent: celui de greffier qui constate et celui de Nestor qui sermonne" (I, p. xx). Both these roles bore him as he reads it over. The sermonising role does not wear well. Twenty-five years later he admits it was abandoned long ago. The Journal had by then become a recreation.

[1] *Pensées de Blaise Pascal*, 2 vols. Paris, Renouard, 1812.

IN SEARCH OF THE SELF

The conception of it as a register persists—the record of a development, of an inner development made in close touch with the whole of contemporary thought. By the third year he calls it his "carnet de voyage" (I, p. 36). Amiel's *Journal Intime* is therefore the diary of an active mind. "It represents", says M. Bouvier, "the action, prolonged for more than thirty years, of a strong and subtle mind which conceived the whole movement of the universe as matter for thought" (I, p. xlvii).[1]

Turn for a moment's digression to the beginning of Stendhal's autobiography (*La Vie de Henri Brulard*): "Je me suis assis sur les marches de San Pietro et là j'ai rêvé une heure ou deux à cette idée. Je vais avoir cinquante ans, il serait bien temps de me connaître. Qu'ai-je été, que suis-je, en vérité je serais bien embarrassé de le dire." The desire to know the self seems irresistible to the restless Beyle. Can the more introspective, the stationary Amiel have escaped it? No; if he takes anything for granted it is this very impulse. From the first it is there, and not just implicitly. If we revert to the most elaborate of his early programmes, this is what we find as the crux of the project: "...—Ma vie la plus centrale, la plus secrète, la plus recueillie.—Relations avec la sphère éternelle.—Expérience intérieure. Conscience de moi..." (I, p. xxii). The tension of inner scrutiny is potentially there. Intermittent in practice, it will occasionally, but with increasing frequency, obsess his faculties and end by producing some of the deepest passages in the Journal.

[1] This applies to the *contents* of Amiel's Journal taken as a whole, not to the specific type of his introspection—a distinction necessary in view of what follows.

Two or three of his conclusions, at least, seem of final importance to our discussion. They point to dead-ends, barriers seemingly impenetrable to the conscious mind, but which this amateur in the psychological quest has clearly discerned. The first is the impasse of self-knowing:

"The consciousness of consciousness is the term and end of analysis. True, but analysis pushed to extremity devours itself, like the Egyptian serpent. We must give it some external matter to crush and dissolve if we wish to prevent its destruction by its action upon itself. 'We are, and ought to be, obscure to ourselves,' said Goethe, 'turned outwards, and working upon the world which surrounds us.' Outward radiation constitutes health; a too continuous concentration upon what is within brings us back to vacuity and blank—an unhealthy state because it effaces us, and others profit by it to keep us effaced. It is better that life should dilate and extend itself in ever-widening circles, than that it should be perpetually diminished and compressed by solitary contraction. Warmth tends to make a globe out of an atom; cold, to reduce a globe to the dimensions of an atom. Analysis has been to me self-annulling, self-destroying" (I, p. 156).[1]

In the second of our chosen passages the *Journal Intime*, used as a diary of mental states and moods, is found to attain not to the self, but to an objective record of its flexibilities and reflections, beyond which the true Subject escapes:

"The intimate journal depersonalises me to such an

[1] I have here used Mrs Humphry Ward's translation, inserting a phrase which she omitted.

extent that I am another person for myself and that I have to make the acquaintance, biographical and moral, of that person. This power of objectivisation becomes a source of forgetfulness. My previous states, my configurations and metamorphoses, escape me like transitory accidents. They become foreign to me, objects of curiosity, contemplation or study; they do not affect my intimate substance; I do not feel them as mine, in me; they are not me. I am not then a will which persists, an activity which accumulates, a consciousness which enriches itself. I am a flexibility which becomes more flexible, an ever-accelerating mutation, the negation of a negation, a reflection throwing itself back and fore as in a pair of confronting mirrors. The narrow mount round each is the only measure of the quantity of reciprocal images which frame themselves indefinitely the one in the other. My identity lies between the 'moi' and the 'toi', but how fluid that makes it!" (II, p. 137).

Now let us ask Amiel: What is the end of the intellectual quest of the self? Here is his reply: "I watch, motionless, my own dismemberment. This Bouddhistic inertia is the proof of intellectualism, of the conversion of all the forces of being into simple reflective consciousness. The meditation of Zero on itself, the vanishing of all phenomena into the substance of the self and of the self into the void, that is the Nirvana of psychology. Nothing perceiving itself, that is what pure thought is" (II, p. 159).

We are left with the inalienable mystery of the self, at which he had hinted twenty years earlier: "Our monad may be influenced by other monads, but none the less it remains impenetrable to them in essence; and we ourselves, when all is said, remain outside our own mystery. The centre of our consciousness is unconscious, as the kernel of the sun is dark. All that we are, desire, do, and know, is more or less superficial, and below the rays and lightnings of our periphery there remains the darkness of unfathomable substance" (I, p. 106).

Amiel's introspection has come full circle and returns to beat on the doors it found closed at the start. True, this paragraph has a sequel which shows that he can perceive the possibility of developments ahead: he actually formulates the Unconscious of modern psychology. But his own self-analysis is at the end of its powers. After the most protracted devotion to the study of the self of which we have a record, the introspection of this investigator is, in its central aim, forced to admit defeat.

There we should have to leave it but for a suggestive comment on the secret of Amiel's defeat, which we have found in the *Extraits d'un Journal* of M. Charles Du Bos.[1] The author, who is best known as a critic, describes himself as a man for whom there is no life without reflection on life. Some passages in his recently published Journal make it possible to claim for him an eminent rank also in the "vocation of introspection". Confessing that the question, Who am I? preoccupies him less than formerly, he differentiates his position from Amiel's in these terms: "Amiel's type of introspection—always prior to the act—seems to me worthless; (whereas) the introspection which follows the act, whether good or bad, seems infinitely fruitful. I know

[1] Corrêa, Paris, 1931.

myself not directly—I tend more and more to believe that one cannot know oneself directly—but through my ecstasies, on one hand, my failures and disasters on the other—and what progress I make is to keep account of both these terms" (p. 326).

M. Du Bos develops his own contribution with the aid of one of Maine de Biran's ideas. To prepare for it let us first glance at this passage from Coleridge's *Anima Poetae* which seems to make the same fundamental distinction.

"By deep feeling we make our *ideas dim*, and this is what we mean by our life, ourselves. I think of the wall —it is before me a distinct image. Here I necessarily think of the *idea* and the thinking *I* as two distinct and opposite things. Now let me think of *myself*, of the thinking being. The idea becomes dim, whatever it be —so dim that I know not what it is; but the feeling is deep and steady, and this I call *I*—identifying the percipient and the perceived."

Maine de Biran's thought is a note to be found in the *Mémoire sur les perceptions obscures*.[1] It may be translated thus: "Each individual is distinguished from another of his species by the fundamental manner in which he feels his life, and consequently in which he *feels*—I do not say in which he judges—his relations to other things, in so far as they can favour or menace his existence. The difference in this respect is perhaps stronger even than that which exists between people's features or the external formation of their bodies. Hence the impossibility with which we are all faced of really *knowing* what one of our fellow-men is as a living and feeling being, and in manifesting what we are ourselves.... Only ideas

[1] Tisserand's edition, p. 21.

resemble one another and can be communicated with the feelings which are attached to them; what belongs to the animal sphere is unknowable."

To Biran's note M. Du Bos joins a phrase from Pater's *Marius*, which refers to the latter's inability to accept "the evaluation of another". M. Du Bos considers *evaluation* to be the most intimate of all acts, the most personal that can be conceived, and beyond rational justification. Biran, he thinks, is not wrong in deriving this act from the animal sphere, which is unknowable. But unknowable, M. Du Bos insists, only in so far as one admits no other mode of knowledge than the rational. His own feeling is that even the "animalité" can rise into lucid consciousness *so long as one does not treat it on the level of discursive analysis*. Systematic introspection, pre-experimental introspection, is vain and yields nothing. But is it the same, he asks, with introspection applied to what, when left to itself, the inner experience brings almost to the surface of our consciousness? Such an avenue of approach has been closed to French philosophers with the exception of Biran and Bergson. They have been paralysed by Descartes's "clear and distinct ideas"; for ideas, as Biran pointed out, belong not to the domain of evaluation but to that of relation.

Confronted by the failure of most methods of introspection, M. Du Bos prefigures a special case from which, it is obvious, he hopes much—"the case when introspection is applied to what comes to the surface in the effervescence of actual composition—not of course what enters into the work itself, but what the accomplishment of the said work teaches us about the complex, half-animal, half-spiritual, which made it possible. That is why, perhaps, there can be no introspectives who are not in some way creators, and this would offer a deeper explanation of the deficiency of Amiel's introspection, which is nothing but a pure introspection, always operating in a state of rest and therefore so often operating on nothing. That too is why there is no greater introspective than Maine de Biran—he who from a purely psychological—not a moral—point of view places the notion of effort in the centre of his philosophy, and places it there because he feels that the faculties in a state of tension yield much more to introspection than when they are relaxed" (pp. 343, 344).

That was written in 1927. The previous year M. André Gide had published in the *Nouvelle Revue Française* his *Journal des Faux-Monnayeurs*. The entries date from 1919 and consist almost entirely of observations on the writing of *Les Faux-Monnayeurs*, which had appeared in 1925. The document is far more the Journal of the novel than of the novelist. No attempt is revealed, along the lines suggested by M. Du Bos, to intercept the self in the act of creation. Rather the *Journal des Faux-Monnayeurs* illustrates the point we made earlier, that the introspection of the artist is dominated as a rule by himself *as artist*. M. Gide leaves us in no doubt as to the purpose of the Journal. It is the *cahier* in which he writes the history of his book, or again in which he stores remarks of a general nature on its basis, composition and *raison d'être*. It is dedicated to those who are interested in questions of craft.

M. Gide's experiment, to which we shall return, raises a point of wider interest. The autobiographical novel has not so far been considered important for this study. It is possible however to believe with M. Ramon Fernandez that the projection of the self into a work of art offers a means of self-knowing superior to direct introspection. In his book, *Messages*, the chapter on "L'autobiographie et le roman", written with reference to the works of Stendhal, presents this case very clearly: "We cannot start from the self for the good reason that we do not know what it is. Christian monadism cannot be more than a mirage in the present state of our knowledge. It is not beside the point to note here that the autobiographies which deserve the name suggest a conception of the self which approximates the latter to non-being rather than to being: the more their analyses are minute and true, the less they succeed in seizing a real unity. Whether it concerns Amiel's 'évanouissements' or the 'effacements sublimes' of Constant, or the 'intermittences' of Proust, it seems that as soon as a great mind tries to seize the self immediately instead of projecting its elements and unifying them in a work or in an action, he exhausts himself in the pursuit of a phantom through the snares which it puts in his path" (pp. 83, 84).

We return to the *Journal des Faux-Monnayeurs* to find some striking illustrations of the truth of this statement. Referring to his own autobiography, *Si le grain ne meurt*,[1] Gide observes: "I was led, while writing it, to think that intimacy, penetration and psychological investigation can, in certain respects, be pushed further in the Novel even than in Confessions. One is sometimes disturbed in the latter by the 'I'; there are certain com-

---

[1] This work, being strictly narrative in form, presents no special interest from our standpoint.

plexities one cannot try to unravel or to reveal without an appearance of complacency" (21st November 1920).

This forestalls M. Fernandez, while it recalls Stendhal's sense of the importunity of the "I", referred to in the preface to *Henri Brulard*. "It is certainly easier for me", Gide notes later on, "to make a character speak than to express myself in my own name, and easier the more the character I create differs from me. I have written nothing better or with more facility than the monologues of Lafcadio or the journal of Alissa. In doing this kind of thing I forget who I am, if I ever knew. I become the other person" (15th November 1923).

When we contrast the intimacy of Alissa's journal in *La Porte Étroite* with the relative objectivity of content and interest in his own published Journals, we perceive what a curious problem Gide's psychology presents from the standpoint of this study. The recent *Pages de Journal*, for instance, reveal far more concern with demonstrating a fixed attitude to the dualism, Communism-Catholicism, than with investigating his mind as it advanced to such a position.

Gide seems to stand somewhere between Amiel and Montaigne. To be placed nearer the latter would be his preference and is, no doubt, his due. What strikes us as common between him and Amiel is first a wide but critical receptivity—something very different from a power of suction like Maeterlinck's. Then there is the attitude to religion, especially the preference they share for Protestantism, but as ideologues not as *pratiquants*. The ultimate indifference each develops to both forms of Christianity is also significant. Above all we find in each the curious ambivalence of the subjective-objective mentality.

Among the greater literary figures in France who have survived Proust, André Gide is probably the most subjective. Externally this might be illustrated from his lifelong collateral cultivation of intimate modes. He speaks in the first person whenever he finds it useful to do so: "Quelle chose absurde, cette crainte de soi, en littérature; crainte de parler de soi, d'intéresser à soi, de se montrer."[1] Yet not only are his dominant works, the majority and the more important, set in objective cadres (novel, drama, *récit*, treatise); even his intimate writings, as we have seen, cannot as a whole be placed under the rubric of introspection. They must go, I think, under ideology. Ideology of a very personal type: the mind thinking thoughts which are its own but always with reference to the "other person", society, humanity, the future (a persistent reality to Gide). And it is this outward reference of an inner reflection which, while it distinguishes him from that other subjectivist, Amiel— making him the psychologist that Amiel never was— assimilates him to the Essayist, his prototype in the habit of thinking the self not in abstraction but in relation:

"Qui ne vit aucunement à autruy, ne vit guere à soy" (III, p. 299).

"J'ay peu me mesler des charges publiques sans me despartir de moy de la largeur d'une ongle, et me donner à autruy sans m'oster à moy" (III, p. 300).

Montaigne emerges, greater in retrospect, cheerful, nonchalant, a happy affront to the "introspective type",

[1] *La Nouvelle Revue Française*, 1st April 1929, p. 499.

superior in wisdom because he looks both ways. These fragments of his gay science suggest that we may retain and perfect our personalities by a judicious balance of inner and outer cultivation—even when we abandon the quest of the "moi" which we have watched his successors pursuing, not without digressions, obstructions and misgivings, through the cells and convolutions of the conscious mind.